Published by Mario's Restaurant
Rochester, New York

Copyright © 2012 by Mario's Restaurant

Library of Congress Cataloging-in-Publication Data
Maytan Jr, Paul.

Mario's: 100 Recipes from the Landmark Rochester, NY Restaurant

p. cm.
Includes Index

ISBN 978-0-9706-2962-3

Printed in Rochester, New York

Printed by Phoenix Graphics, 2012

For more information on Mario's Pasta Sauce,
Mario's Pretzellini or Mario's Restaurant
www.Mariosit.com

Mario's Restaurant and Catering
2740 Monroe Avenue
Rochester, NY 14618
585-271-1111
info@mariosit.com

Mario's

Recipes & Text
Paul Maytan Jr.

Photography
Matt Wittmeyer & Sharon Merisola Yockel

Forward
Anthony Daniele

From Left to Right, Anthony, Erin, Bridget, Lauren, Michael, Caleb, April, Grace and Danny Daniele

Contents

Forward

Passion. Integrity. Profit. Being the son of a charismatic, talented man like Mario, certainly has its challenges. The lessons my brother and I have learned are far too many to even list here. Our journey, as a family, has been a remarkably rewarding one. One we have been blessed to flourish in and sincerely enjoy. The most significant lesson demonstrated so well by our father, is Savor the joy in making other people happy. In turn, you will find the same happiness if not more. And don't forget you have to make a buck along the way.

Danny, Mario and Anthony Daniele

Since we were just old enough to see over the front counter, the restaurant business has been the center of our lives. Mornings, weekends, holidays and every night smelling that herb roll smell on every coat and shirt in the closet. The best part was always recounting the many stories, not all appropriate, not all pleasant, but certainly interesting. Most significantly, the stories that included someone's 90th birthday, a first communion, rehearsal dinners, the small and large moments in other's lives that they chose to allow us to make extra special. My father took such pride in those parties. He would laugh, cry, make toasts, to the point of embarrassing us as we reminded him we were not a part of their family. His response, *"we are today!"*, and in many cases, we still are, ten, twenty and thirty years later.

The relationships and lifelong effect our businesses have had are not unique to the millions of guests who have walked through the doors, but include the thousands of employees who, through the years, have themselves become what "Mario's" is all about. Employees, who started as teenagers washing dishes in the late 80's and are managers today. Staff whose children have worked for us on school breaks. Spending nearly half of our lives together, shoulder to shoulder, on some of the most hectic and seemingly impossible nights in the restaurant business. Our father made it very clear, don't expect your employee to do anything you wouldn't or couldn't do yourself.

The business that shaped our childhood has also shaped our adulthood. I met my wife when I was twelve, cashiering at the front counter with my mother. She would come in every Friday with her family, parents on both sides giggling and encouraging us to say hi to each other. Well we finally did and now our thirteen year old daughter is hostessing, our eleven year old son dons a chef coat and hat to prepare waffles on Sunday. Our youngest is chomping at the bit to get her chance at bartending, already an expert crafter of the Shirley Temple.

This book is full of flavor, but more importantly, magic moments for you and your loved ones to make a meal into something much more. Buon Appetito.

Anthony Daniele

The story of Mario's

Our story really begins 65 years ago in a tiny mountain village in the Italian region of Abruzzi when Mario Daniele was born to Querino and Esilde Daniele. By the age of fourteen Mario had already established his first business, opening the first appliance store in the area surrounding his hometown of Castelnuovo. He also sold the local black truffles and saffron that was grown by family members and their neighbors to grocery stores and restaurants throughout the region. This was Mario's first exposure to the food business.

In that era, it was mandatory for young Italian men to serve 18 months in the military so at eighteen he was placed in Aeronautica, the Italian Air Force where due to his natural, mechanical inclination he served as a specialized machinery mechanic. Eight months into his service he was sent to Canada and on February 1st, 1967, a date he well remembers, he first set foot on North American soil, eventually ending up in Windsor, Ontario, Canada, just across the border from Detroit, Michigan, where he would remain until his discharge.

In 1969 while visiting his paternal uncles in Rochester, NY, he met his future wife Flora. Several families from Castelnuovo had immigrated to the Rochester area including Flora's family. Coincidentally, they went to the first and second grade together in Italy before she moved to the United States when she was just eight years old. After a year of commuting to Rochester from Windsor, Mario proposed to Flora. They were married July 12, 1969.

Mario also had relatives in Detroit including his cousin John Zaccagnini and the Tringali family who had a small chain of three restaurants called Mama Mia's. At night Flora and Mario would often go there to spend time with family. It was this continued

Mario's Pizzeria, Farmington Hills, MI 1972

contact with the restaurant business that inspired him, in 1969, to open his first *Mario's Pizzeria* in Farmington Hills, Detroit.

The pizzeria was an immediate success, largely due to Mario and Flora working seven days a week, taking only Thanksgiving and Christmas day off. In the early days and when business was slow Mario would prepare a dozen pizzas at a time and take them around the neighborhood offering to sell them at a discounted price. Never once did he return with unsold pizza. It was there he first recreated the sauce his mother had made for him in Italy years before and also where he came up the idea of *Spaghetti in a Bucket* selling spaghetti and meatballs in 1.5-gallon pails. These were very popular with his customers.

The pizzeria business thrived and afforded Mario the opportunity to purchase a 125-acre farm in Fowlerville, Michigan in partnership with his cousins. He subsequently subdivided the farm into 10-acre parcels and sold them all. This allowed him to eventually purchase the small shopping center that held his pizzeria and an A&P grocery store. He vividly recalls his lawyer admonishing him that the monthly payment on the real estate was higher than the gross revenue of the pizzeria. But he quickly developed, subdivided and leased out the building and once established, it became a success as a small shopping center. It was during his time in Detroit that he became an American citizen, sponsored by his good friend Frank Guidobono. It was also during the Detroit years that his two sons, first Anthony in 1971 and then Danny in 1974 were born.

In the mid seventies the Zaccagnini and Tringali families, decided to move to Florida. Mario and family lingered in Michigan for another year before deciding, since there was no longer any immediate family to share time with, to move to Rochester, New York. Mario's uncles were still there and several cousins as well as Flora's mother, sister and brother. He sold the pizzeria but retained the commercial property.

Once he arrived in Rochester, Mario was eager to get back into business and he soon found himself partnering to take over the landmark *Carriage Stop* restaurant and banquet facility, which at the time this was one of Rochester's most popular eateries. Known

Mario's Pizza & Pasta, Rochester, NY 1981

for having the longest bar in the city the Carriage Stop had even more square footage than the current Mario's. They were serving five-to-six hundred dinners a night with live music five nights a week and one or two weddings every Saturday. After about a year of this, Flora told Mario that she had enough of raising the two boys practically alone while he worked seemingly endlessly. So Mario sold his half of the *Carriage Stop* thinking he would get out of the restaurant business completely.

Despite Flora's requests, Mario would close out the decade by opening another *Mario's*. It was a small pizzeria located on Monroe Avenue, intended to keep him busy while he was figuring out what he was going to do next. It wasn't long, however, before another restaurant opportunity presented itself. He recalls making wine in his garage when the president of *Pizza Kitchen* on East Avenue called to ask him if he would mind taking a look at the restaurant and offer an opinion about the value of the business. The place looked beautiful and when Mario was told he could have the place for half of what he had judged the value to be, he jumped at the chance to obtain it. This restaurant, on East Avenue near downtown, became the now legendary *Mario's Pizza and Pasta*.

The East Avenue Restaurant was widely successful. Mario soon established a following community wide. People flocked to the place in droves from all over Monroe County. He attributes this success to one basic principle, customer satisfaction, which has always been his number one priority. This extended to all aspects of the business, even the sauce recipes, the cornerstones of any Italian kitchen, were developed strictly on the basis of what his customers told him they liked.

Mario's ultimate signature item was the hard crust herb rolls. People would wait in line for the next batch of freshly baked rolls to be delivered to the wicker basket at the end of the salad bar. It was not uncommon to see customers juggling the piping hot rolls on the way back to their table but not before slathering Mario's magic butter on them first. He continually focused on high quality fresh ingredients and good customer relations making it a point to visit each table to personally thank his customers for their patronage, and he regularly provided free wine to customers who had been waiting too long for their table to ensure that no guest ever minded waiting to be seated.

Considering the fact that he had no formal training Mario became an outstanding cook, possessed with great culinary instincts and a passion for the food of his homeland. He always understood the importance of putting flavor first. It was his business acumen, however, that really catapulted his success and over the years he would come to rely more and more on his Chefs and kitchen staff to prepare the food while he continued to develop the business. The first to take the reins from Mario was Chef Paolino Bernabei, another Abruzzese native, who headed up the East Ave. kitchen for several years.

Mario's Pizza & Pasta continued to be successful for over eighteen years before closing its doors for the last time on New Year's Day 1997. Several years earlier Anthony and Danny, who were both in college at the time pursuing business degrees, told their father that they wanted to remain in the restaurant business. The lease for the building that *Mario's Pizza & Pasta* occupied was due to expire and since there was no opportunity to buy the property, Mario decided mainly upon the urging of his sons, to obtain the land necessary to construct the existing building that the current *Mario's* restaurant occupies today.

A concept for a new restaurant to be called *Mario's-Via Abruzzi*, which translated means, Mario's-by way of Abruzzi, was developed, and after several months of market research a location was decided upon. Mario had always wanted to own a restaurant that produced nothing but authentic Italian cuisine, specifically that of the Abruzzi region and the timing seemed perfect given the fact that Northern and Regional Italian Restaurants were the hottest trend in the industry at the time. Even if that meant letting go of the ever popular but somewhat dated salad bar and some of the other things that made *Mario's Pizza & Pasta* so popular. It was also the first time in Rochester's history that an individual operating out of a small business was able to secure the funding for a large multi-million dollar project. This feat would help earn him *Rochester Entrepreneur* magazine's *Business Man of the Year* award in 1995.

On July 1st, 1995 *Mario's-Via Abruzzi* officially opened its doors to the public. Everything from the décor, bedecked with Italian marble, to the menu, showcasing regional Italian dishes and Abruzzese specialties, right down to the architecture of the building was designed to bring the authentic Italian experience to Rochester. The restaurant would be hailed as a triumph by the public and media alike. People were literally lining up around the building to "check out Mario's new place."

But success came at a price. While the restaurant was resounding success, what looked like a beautiful swan sailing gracefully above the water was in reality paddling like mad just beneath the surface. The restaurant was open for lunch and dinner seven days a week and it was so busy that sometimes people waiting in line for lunch did not get seated until dinner! It seemed impossible at times to keep up, plus there was still another restaurant to run! That first year at *Mario's-Via Abruzzi* proved to be beyond stressful but failure was never an option. Within a year things were running smoothly. The chaos that would come to define year one proved to be a steep, but important, learning curve that would provide priceless experience as the company expanded into other restaurant ventures a few years later.

Mario's-Via Abruzzi, Rochester, NY 1995

Expansion was never in doubt once Anthony and Danny joined forces with Mario. In 2001 *Bazil-A Casual Italian Kitchen* opened on East Henrietta Road. The intent was to bring back *Mario's Pizza & Pasta* casual style dining back since *Mario's-Via Abruzzi* had become something of a special occasion restaurant. This would later prompt, in effort to more clearly differentiate the two restaurants, an emphasis on top quality steaks and a name change from *Mario's-Via Abruzzi* to *Mario's Italian Steakhouse and Catering*. The new *Mario's* was a fusion of classic NY style steakhouse and Italian fare with most of the signature steak dishes having a distinctive Italian flair. This would prove to be a successful change that ran for several years until the *Italian Steakhouse* moniker was dropped in a favor of the simpler and more timeless *Mario's*. Although there would be less of an emphasis on steaks, the menu stayed pretty much the same thematically but it became smaller so there could be more focus on the quality of each individual menu item.

In 2003 Mario's decided to market his marinara sauce. Chef Paolino Bernabei was nearing retirement age and in the interest of consistency *Cantisano Foods*, now *LiDestri Foods*, was brought in to see if they could duplicate that recipe. After several test batches failed to match Mario's sauce they were eventually able to duplicate it and the sauce was bottled, originally in gallon jugs for use at the restaurants, and later in retail sized jars sold as *Mario's Pasta Sauce*. *Vodka Sauce*, and *Three Cheese Marinara* were later added to the sauce line. Mario's pasta sauces are now sold in over 1,500 stores throughout the Northeast. In 2009 Mario's Pretzellini, an edible centerpiece made from seasoned fried pasta was added to Mario's product line.

A second identical *Bazil* was built from scratch on Irondequoit Bay in September 2006 with an attached Marina complex called *The Southpoint Marina*. This would prove to be the more successful of the two *Bazil* locations and sensing the need in Rochester for a seafood restaurant the first *Bazil* was remodeled and changed to *The Original Crab Shack* in 2010. The *Crab Shack* was voted *Rochester's Best New Restaurant* by the readers of *City Magazine* later that year.

Over the years Mario's restaurants have come out on top numerous times in *Best of Rochester* polls conducted by both *City Magazine* and the *Democrat & Chronicle*. Mario credits this to his continued dedication to customer satisfaction as well as his ability to attract and maintain staff members that share this philosophy. The same dedication he brought back when he opened his first pizzeria he, Anthony and Danny still bring today. Mario's now famous slogan, *"You are not just a customer, you are my special guest,"* is not just a catchy phrase, it's a way of doing business.

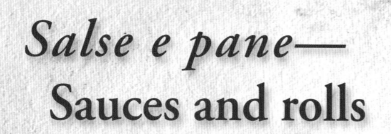

Salse e pane—
Sauces and rolls

Piazza of Castelnuovo, Abruzzo, Italy

Mario's *marinara*

INGREDIENTS *3 lb plum tomatoes ‖ 2 (28 oz) cans crushed tomatoes ‖ 2 (10 oz) cans tomato paste ‖ ½ cup extra-virgin olive oil ‖ 1 cup chopped onion ‖ ½ cup chopped garlic ‖ ½ bay leaf ‖ ½ cup white wine ‖ ½ cup fresh basil, packed ‖ 1½ teaspoon sugar ‖ 1 pinch baking soda ‖ To taste, Kosher salt and freshly ground black pepper*

ONE Wash the fresh plum tomatoes. Set up a grinder attachment on a Kitchen-Aid or similar appliance. Run the tomatoes through the grinder using a medium-sized die. Separately, run the garlic through the grinder. **TWO** Heat the oil in a large heavy-bottomed pot over medium heat for 2-3 minutes. Add the garlic and allow it to fry until it browns and obtains a cardboard color. The garlic should sizzle when it hits the pan. Quickly add the onions and bay leaf and stir to combine. The water released from the onions will prevent the garlic from continuing to brown or burn. Continue to sauté until the onions soften. **THREE** Add the wine and simmer briefly before adding the tomato products, basil, sugar, and baking soda. Simmer over low heat, stirring occasionally, for an additional 30 minutes to allow the flavors to develop. This sauce should retain some of its freshness and therefore does not require extended cooking.

Makes 3 quarts

Alfredo sauce

INGREDIENTS *2½ quarts light cream ‖ 1¼ stick unsalted butter ‖ 1 cup all-purpose flour ‖ 4 oz ham ‖ 1 small clove garlic, sliced ‖ 1 cup parmigiano-reggiano or grana-padana cheese, grated ‖ 1 cup shredded asiago cheese, good quality ‖ To taste, Kosher salt and white pepper*

ONE Bring the light cream to a boil. **TWO** In a separate pot, melt the butter over medium heat. Add the onions, ham, and garlic. Sauté until the onions soften. Turn the heat down to a low setting and add the flour. Cook the mixture over low heat for ten minutes stirring occasionally to thicken the sauce, forming a roux. **THREE** Add the cream and simmer over medium heat for 30 minutes. Add the parmesan and asiago cheeses and season with salt and white pepper. Combine until most of the cheese has melted and strain to remove the ham, garlic and un-melted cheese.

Makes 3 quarts

MARIO'S SAUCES These sauces were developed by Mario Daniele. It took many months of trial-and-error but ultimately it was customer feedback that determined what the final sauce recipes would be.

Vodka sauce

INGREDIENTS *1 batch recipe Mario's marinara sauce* ‖ *1 quart heavy cream* ‖ *2 cups vodka* ‖ *1 cup dry white wine* ‖ *¼ teaspoon crushed red pepper* ‖ *1 cup grana-padana cheese, grated quality* ‖ *8 oz unsalted butter* ‖ *Kosher salt and white pepper to taste*

ONE Prepare a batch of Mario's marinara sauce. **TWO** Bring the cream to a boil in an oversized heavy-bottomed pot over high heat. As the cream boils it will reduce in volume and thicken. Continue to boil until the cream has thickened to a sauce-like consistency. **THREE** Add the reduced cream, vodka, white wine, parmesan cheese, and crushed red pepper to the marinara and stir to combine. Simmer for 15 minutes over low heat to allow the flavors to develop and the cheese to melt. Stir in the butter to finish.

Makes 3½ quarts

Abruzzi style fresh tomato sauce

INGREDIENTS *5 lb ripe plum tomatoes* ‖ *2 cups extra-virgin olive oil* ‖ *3 tablespoons fresh garlic, chopped* ‖ *⅓ cup shallots, finely chopped* ‖ *3 ounces fresh basil, torn into small pieces, or chopped* ‖ *To taste, crushed red pepper or hot pepper pods* ‖ *To taste, Kosher salt and freshly ground black pepper*

ONE Using a paring knife, cut a small x in the top of the tomatoes. Submerge them in boiling water for about one minute or until the skins begin to blister. Remove and cool them down in ice water. Peel and cut in half. Gently squeeze out the seeds and chop. **TWO** Heat the oil in a large skillet over high heat. Add the garlic and fry, stirring often, until the garlic becomes brown. Be careful not to burn. The garlic should be evenly colored and slightly darker than cardboard or cork. Remove any part of the garlic that has been burned. Add the shallots, hot pepper and about half of the basil. Fry briefly until the shallots begin to soften. The water released from the shallots will prevent the garlic from continuing to brown. **THREE** Add the tomatoes and continue to fry until they are *just* cooked. Add the remaining basil and extra-virgin olive oil to finish. Season to taste with Kosher salt and freshly ground black pepper.

Makes 3 quarts

IT'S ALL ABOUT THE GARLIC This memorable-tasting fresh tomato sauce gets its unique flavor from browning the garlic in hot olive oil. In this way, the pungency of the garlic is muted, while the flavor is intensified.

Mario's hard crust herb rolls

This recipe was converted from the much larger batch recipe that we used at both *Mario's Pizza & Pasta* and *Mario's Via Abruzzi*. In a professional kitchen we weigh the flour using a baker's scale, which we suspect is not an option for many people at home. Be advised you will get better, more consistent results if you weigh the flour. This recipe for rolls is also the same one we used for pizza dough. For best results making homemade pizza, crank your oven up to 500° F and place a pizza stone on the bottom rack.

INGREDIENTS *7 cups (2 lb) all-purpose flour, sifted then measured* ‖ *16 fl oz warm tap water (about 90° F)* ‖ *3 tablespoons Butter Flavored Crisco shortening* ‖ *½ oz dry active yeast* ‖ *4 teaspoons salt, iodized* ‖ *1 teaspoons granulated garlic* ‖ *½ teaspoon ground black pepper* ‖ *½ teaspoon dried oregano* ‖ *½ teaspoon ground oregano* ‖ *½ teaspoon dried parsley* ‖ *Melted butter, as needed to brush on the rolls* ‖ *Oil or pan-spray, as needed to grease the baking pan*

ONE Carefully measure out the yeast, salt, granulated garlic, ground pepper, ground oregano and dried oregano into a small bowl. Measure the shortening. Sift and measure the flour or, preferably weigh the flour. **TWO** Add the warm tap water, shortening, and butter to the bowl of a Kitchen-Aid or other tabletop mixer fitted with a dough hook. Mix briefly to help melt the shortening and butter. Add the dry ingredients and mix briefly to incorporate. **THREE** Add the flour and run the mixer for about three minutes or until the dough forms into a ball and pulls away from the sides of the mixer. **FOUR** Empty the dough onto a clean lightly floured surface. Cut and pull it into roughly 1½ inch, diameter "log" shapes. Cut across these log shapes to form rolls roughly 2-3 inches in size. Place the rolls on a pre-oiled baking pan and brush a dab of melted butter onto each one. **FIVE** Proof rolls by first placing an oven thermometer in the oven and turning it on for a few minutes. Once the oven gets to about 90° F place a shallow pan of hot tap water on the bottom shelf. This will provide a warm humid environment suitable for proofing. Put the rolls in the oven and when they have just about doubled in size they are ready to bake. **SIX** Bake in a preheated 350° F oven (preferably using fan assisted convection heat) for 15 minutes or until they are done.

Makes 18 rolls

THE STUFF OF LEGEND At *Mario's Pizza & Pasta* these rolls were the stuff of legend as people would line up waiting for the freshly baked rolls to be brought out, straight from the oven to the salad bar. Guests were often seen juggling the piping hot rolls on the way back to their tables.

Antipasti—
Appetizers

From Left to Right, Mario Daniele, age 25; Anthony, Mario, Fabio & Danny Daniele 1982; Flora Daniele, age 17

Fried calamari

American foodies possess all sorts of kitchen gadgetry, so a deep fryer is not at all uncommon in today's home kitchen. Temperature control is important for effective frying and it's very easy to get good results with a deep fryer since the temperature is thermostatically controlled. If you don't have a deep fryer, an electric wok or even an electric frying pan will also work very well. You can also heat up the oil in a pan on the stove, but for dependable results it's a good idea to have a clip-on frying thermometer handy.

INGREDIENTS *3 lb whole squid or 2½ lb cleaned squid tubes and tentacles* ‖ *1½ cup all-purpose flour* ‖ *Frying oil or shortening for deep frying as needed* ‖ *6 egg whites* ‖ *To taste, sea salt and freshly ground pepper, to taste* ‖ *1 lemon, cut into six wedges* ‖ *1 cup, Mario's marinara (see page 2) or 1 jar Mario's Pasta Sauce*

ONE Clean the squid, if not already cleaned. Pull and discard the long strand from the tentacle cluster. Remove the quill and any membranes from the inside of the tubes and rinse. Cut the tubes into ½ inch wide rings. **TWO** Fill an electric fryer (or other suitable pan) with at least 4 inches of oil. Heat the oil to 350° F and set to maintain the temperature. **THREE** Separate the egg whites from 6 eggs. Whisk together the egg whites. Add the squid and salt and pepper to taste. Add the flour and toss with the squid to coat them thoroughly. Transfer to a wire strainer and shake off the excess flour. **FOUR** Fry until the coating has begun to get crispy and the squid are just starting to shrink, which should take less than 1 minute. Remove with a slotted spoon, drain and serve promptly, with lemon wedges and heated sauce for dipping.

Serves 6

SQUIDELICIOUS! Fried and grilled calamari have, hands down, been our most popular appetizers at *Mario's* over the years. We go through an average of 200 pounds of squid per week. That's over 10,000 pounds a year!

Grilled calamari

Techniques that bring out and enhance the natural flavor of food is what good cooking is all about. Here we dust the squid with oiled, seasoned breadcrumbs and cook them quickly on a char-grill. The breadcrumbs char very quickly, which gives a nice char-grilled flavor to the dish without overcooking the squid, a feat that would otherwise be impossible. This dish has been a staple on our menu since 1998.

INGREDIENTS *3 lb whole squid or 2½ lb cleaned squid tubes and tentacles* ‖ *1 cup extra-virgin olive oil* ‖ *2 fresh lemons, cut into wedges* ‖ *1½ cup plain breadcrumbs* ‖ *1 tablespoon Italian parsley, chopped* ‖ *To taste, sea salt and freshly ground black pepper*

ONE Clean the squid, if not already cleaned. Pull and discard the long strand from the tentacle cluster. Remove the quill and any membranes from the inside of the tubes and rinse. Cut several slits into the tubes, about three-fourth of the way through, so that laying flat the tube resembles a wide-toothed comb. **TWO** Season the breadcrumbs to taste with salt and pepper and combine with the olive oil. **THREE** Combine the juice of 1 lemon and about half of the olive oil. Season lightly with sea salt and pepper. This will serve as a marinade as well as to bond the breadcrumbs to the squid. Marinate the squid in this mixture for at least 30 minutes. **FOUR** Pre-heat your gas or charcoal grill. Toss the squid in the breadcrumbs to coat evenly. Grill the squid for two minutes, turning occasionally to avoid burning. The calamari should be *just* done when removed from the grill. It's only a matter of a minute before they become overcooked and overcooked squid are tough and chewy. **FIVE** Transfer the squid to a serving platter and drizzle the remaining olive oil over it. Serve with fresh lemon wedges.

Serves 6

ROCHESTER'S FIRST We don't like to name-drop (or brag), but we don't think it's a coincidence that we've seen this dish on several menus around town since we introduced it back in 1998. Don't be fooled by the imitators! Mario was preparing squid like this 50 years ago in Abruzzi.

Garlic shrimp

The garlic butter we use at Mario's is one of our signature recipes. We use it as a compound butter to finish steaks and seafood as well as for garlic bread and in scampi-style dishes. What makes it special is the subtle addition of bleu cheese, not enough that you can taste it mind you, but enough to give the butter a unique depth of flavor. This recipe calls for the shrimp to be served with bread as an appetizer but you could easily turn this into an entrée by serving it over pasta.

INGREDIENTS *24 large raw shrimp ‖ 2 lemons cut into wedges ‖ ⅓ cup extra-virgin olive oil ‖ 1½ cups garlic gutter ‖ ¼ cup dry white wine ‖ To taste, sea salt and freshly ground pepper ‖ 1 loaf Italian bread, such as ciabatta or filone*

GARLIC BUTTER *12 ounces unsalted butter ‖ ⅓ cup fresh garlic cloves, chopped ‖ ½ cup bleu cheese crumbles ‖ ¼ cup scallions, chopped ‖ ¼ cup Italian parsley, chopped ‖ To taste, Kosher salt and freshly ground pepper*

ONE Peel and de-vein the shrimp if they are not already cleaned. **TWO** For the garlic butter: Cream the bleu cheese in a food processor and transfer to a Kitchen-Aid bowl or other mixing bowl. Add the butter, garlic, scallions, salt and pepper. Whip on high speed for about 5 minutes or until the butter is light and airy. Add the parsley and combine. Do not add the parsley until the last minute because it will turn the butter green. **THREE** Heat the olive oil in a large sauté pan over medium heat. Season the shrimp to taste with salt and pepper and add them to the pan. Toss until the shrimp's appearance changes from translucent to opaque/white. Add the white wine to the pan, then the garlic butter and continue to cook until the butter has *just* melted and is still foamy. **FOUR** Serve with grilled or toasted Italian bread and fresh lemon wedges.

Serves 6

IT'S NOT SHRIMP SHRIMP! Scampi is not the Italian word for shrimp as is commonly misunderstood in America. Actually, *scampi* (plural) or *scampo* (singular) are not shrimp at all. They are a shellfish species that is similar to langoustines or Dublin Bay prawns. Meaning, in terms of taste and appearance, they are more like tiny lobsters than shrimp. In some parts of Italy, it is traditional to flavor scampi with garlic and butter, which is why American-Italian restaurants that prepare shrimp this way tend to call the dish shrimp scampi or *alla scampi*.

Grilled shrimp wrapped in pancetta with arugula

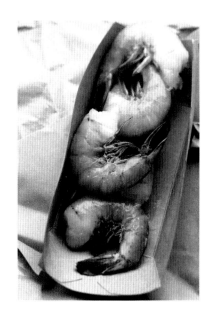

If you are unfamiliar with pancetta, think of it as a slab of bacon that's rolled up and air cured instead of smoked like American bacon. You can purchase pre-sliced pancetta, unroll the slices and wrap them like American bacon around shrimp. In this recipe, we wrap the shrimp with a generous amount of arugula. Pancetta is used in a variety of ways to deepen the flavor of countless dishes. It is one of the essential ingredients in an Italian kitchen.

INGREDIENTS *18 raw shrimp* ‖ *18 slices, pancetta (about 6 oz)* ‖ *2 oz arugula* ‖ *½ cup extra-virgin olive oil* ‖ *1 lemon, cut into wedges* ‖ *To taste, sea salt and freshly ground pepper*

ONE Peel and de-vein the shrimp if they are not already cleaned. Place the shrimp in a bowl and season to taste with salt and pepper. **TWO** Place a few arugula leaves onto the center of each slice. Carefully wrap the pancetta and arugula together around each shrimp. Cover as much of the shrimp as possible with the pancetta and secure with a toothpick. **THREE** Pre-heat your gas or charcoal grill. Place the shrimp on the grill and turn as needed to obtain grill marks. Continue to cook until the shrimp are *just* done, meaning they have *just* turned from translucent to opaque. **FOUR** Serve drizzled with extra-virgin olive oil and fresh lemon wedges.

Serves 6

CLEANING SHRIMP Raw shrimp are usually sold *shell-on*, which means there is going to be some prep work involved because you will want to remove the shells and clean out the entrails. Start by peeling away the shell, beginning at the head end (the end opposite of the tail) and working your way up to the tail. Once the shell is removed, lay the shrimp on its side and carefully cut a small slit across the length of the topside. At this point you should be able to remove the entrails or *veins* with your fingers. Rinse any remaining debris by holding the shrimp under a little running water. Save the shells because they can later be used to make shrimp or seafood stock.

Oil poached shrimp with tangerine and horseradish-avocado sauce

We developed this recipe for a special occasion menu. Here the shrimp are slow poached in olive oil, a contemporary poaching method. We serve it with horseradish-avocado sauce, a nice alternative to cocktail sauce, and dress it up with tangerine sections and a colorful micro-greens salad.

INGREDIENTS *18 large raw shrimp ‖ 3 tangerines, seedless ‖ ½ each red, yellow and green pepper ‖ 1 red onion ‖ 2 cups extra-virgin olive oil, for poaching plus 3 fl oz for dressing ‖ 2 cups salad oil ‖ ¼ cup champagne vinegar, or white vinegar ‖ ½ pint micro-greens, available at good grocery stores ‖ To taste, sea salt and white pepper to taste*

HORSERADISH-AVOCADO SAUCE *2 ripe California avocados ‖ 1 tablespoon horseradish, drained ‖ ½ cup sour cream ‖ ¼ cup mayonnaise ‖ 1 lemon, juiced ‖ To taste, sea salt and white pepper*

ONE Peel the tangerines and separate the sections, taking care to separate most of the skin and pith (white part). Peel and thinly julienne the onions. Cut the peppers in half, remove the piths, and cut them into fine julienne strips. Submerge the onions and peppers in ice water for two hours. **TWO** Put the olive oil and salad oil together in a large pot. Attach a deep-fry thermometer to the side of the saucepan and heat the oils over medium heat until the thermometer registers between 165° F and 180° F. Add the shrimp to the warm oil and poach for 6-8 minutes or until they are opaque in the center. Remove the shrimp from the oil and set onto paper towels to drain. When the shrimp are cool enough to handle, peel and de-vein them. **THREE** To make the horseradish-avocado sauce: Cut the avocados in half, remove the seeds and scoop out the inside. Put the avocado in a blender or food processor and add the horseradish, sour cream, mayonnaise and the juice of 1 lemon. Pulse to obtain a smooth texture. Season to taste with sea salt and white pepper. **FOUR** Drain the peppers and onions and dry them using a paper towel. Put them in a bowl together with the micro-greens and lightly dress the mixture with olive oil and good quality champagne vinegar. **FIVE** Arrange three shrimp on a plate with the horseradish-avocado sauce. Place 3-4 tangerine wedges on the shrimp. Top the shrimp with the micro-greens salad and serve with horseradish-avocado sauce.

Serves 6

OIL-POACHING The thing that makes oil poaching different from frying or sautéing in oil is the fact that you are keeping the temperature low enough so that the shrimp poach slowly. This will keep them moist, succulent, and evenly cooked throughout. This technique is great for shrimp, scallops, lobster, and delicate whitefish.

Baked oysters with artichoke & sun-dried tomato stuffing

Oysters, or *ostriche,* were popular among the ancient Romans, who for centuries had them brought in from the famed oyster beds of Taranto in Southern Italy. The popularity of oysters has not waned through two millennia, but these days most of the oysters served in Italy are brought over from France. Make sure to hydrate the sun-dried tomatoes with a little warm water otherwise they have a tendency to burn.

INGREDIENTS *24 live oysters* ‖ *4 slices pancetta, chopped* ‖ *1 (10 oz) can quartered artichokes, coarsely chopped* ‖ *10 slices Italian bread* ‖ *1 large egg* ‖ *3 tablespoons unsalted butter* ‖ *⅓ cup extra-virgin olive oil* ‖ *1 cup onion, chopped* ‖ *1 tablespoon Italian parsley, chopped* ‖ *2 oz sun-dried tomatoes, chopped and moistened with warm tap water* ‖ *1 lemon, cut into wedges*

ONE Set the bread onto a baking sheet and place in a 325° F oven for 8-10 minutes, to toast and dry the bread. Set out to cool. **TWO** Heat the olive oil in a sauté pan over medium heat. Add the pancetta and cook for 5-6 minutes until the pancetta begins to brown, rendering out some of the fat. Add the butter, onion, and parsley and continue to cook until the onions soften. **THREE** Cut the bread slices into small cubes and add them to the pan together with the artichokes, sun-dried tomatoes, and egg. Mix to combine. **FOUR** Scrub and shuck the oysters and drain any excess juices into the stuffing mix. Place the oysters onto a baking sheet and top them with the stuffing. Bake in a 350° F preheated oven for 6 minutes. Serve with fresh lemon wedges.

Serves 6

OYSTERS AND ROCK SALT The photo shows the oysters on a bed of rock salt. This fancy touch, common in upscale restaurants, is rooted in the ancient practice of cooking oysters on pebbles. The pebbles kept the oysters from tipping and losing their juices while keeping the shells warm.

Fresh oysters with saffron mignonette

Oysters are reputed to have aphrodisiac properties and for this reason we always find some way of incorporating them into our Valentine's Day menu. People don't normally think of saffron when they are dressing an oyster but trust us on this one, once you've tried this saffron infused mignonette it will be your favorite way to eat them.

INGREDIENTS *24 live oysters* ‖ *⅔ cup rice wine vinegar* ‖ *¼ cup chopped shallots* ‖ *2 tablespoons freshly cracked black pepper or mixed cracked peppercorns* ‖ *1 pinch saffron* ‖ *To taste, sea salt*

ONE To make the saffron mignonette: Put the vinegar, shallots, cracked pepper, salt and saffron in a non-reactive saucepan. Simmer over high heat for 1 minute to allow the saffron to steep into the vinegar. Refrigerate to cool down. **TWO** Scrub and shuck the oysters, separating the oyster meat completely from the shells without loosing any more of the natural juices than necessary. Serve them topped with some of the mignonette.

Serves 6

CHOOSING AND CLEANING OYSTERS When choosing oysters look for them to be tightly closed and not chipped or broken. Steer clear of displays that look dried out or that contain several open oysters already as these are probably nearing the end of their shelf life. Store them with the larger, deeper half shell side down, covered with wet paper towel. To clean them, scrub shells using a bristle brush under a little cold running water.

Mussels in saffron and tomato broth

In Abruzzi, a typical seaboard restaurant will offer a half dozen or more different seafood antipasti. These are brought to the table and passed around family style, similar to the way most of us would at home. A big steaming bowl of fresh mussels is perfect for this kind of meal.

INGREDIENTS *3 lb black mussels ‖ 6 cups water ‖ 1 teaspoon saffron threads ‖ 2 cups plum tomatoes, chopped ‖ 3 tablespoons shallots, chopped fine ‖ 2 tablespoons, garlic, chopped fine ‖ ½ cup fresh basil, chopped ‖ 2 teaspoon fresh parsley, chopped ‖ 1 teaspoon fresh thyme, stripped from the stem and chopped ‖ 1 teaspoon fresh rosemary, stripped from the stem and chopped ‖ 1 cup extra-virgin olive oil ‖ To taste, sea salt and freshly ground pepper*

ONE Chop the tomatoes or using a paring knife, cut a small x in the top of the tomatoes. Submerge them in boiling water for about one minute or until the skins begin to blister. Remove and cool them down in ice water. Peel and cut in half. Gently squeeze out the seeds and chop. **TWO** Put all the ingredients into a large pot over medium-high heat and simmer until the mussels open. Remove and discard unopened mussels and serve mussels with tomatoes and broth in large bowls. We like to serve this accompanied with grilled slices of crusty Italian bread.

Serves 6

SEAFOOD ANTIPASTI AT LA MURENA One of our favorite restaurants is *La Murena* in Pescara, Abruzzi. On our first staff trip to Italy, we were served these mussels along with steamed periwinkles in a rosemary-tomato broth, fish meatballs, sautéed clams with garlic, and steamed Scampi. This was just the first course! These offerings arrived at the table piping hot on serving platters and in bowls, which were passed around family style-just like at home.

Salmon carpaccio

Cured salmon (aka lox) is best for this dish. You can cure your own salmon using a mixture of salt, sugar, and a flavoring ingredient like dill or pickling spices or you can purchase salmon that is already cured that is also pre-sliced. In this dish, we lay out the salmon just like you would for a beef carpaccio, dress it with lemon vinaigrette, and garnish with thinly cut gherkins and a chiffonade of arugula. You could also roll the salmon for a different presentation. This recipe is a favorite on our holiday brunches.

INGREDIENTS *1½-2 lb cured or smoked salmon, pre-sliced ‖ 3 oz arugula, cut into thin chiffonade strips ‖ 12 gherkin pickles (sweet pickles), sliced ‖ 1 lemon, very thinly sliced and seeds removed ‖ ½ cup extra-virgin olive oil ‖ 2 lemons, juiced ‖ To taste, sea salt fresh ground pepper*

ONE Make lemon vinaigrette by whisking together extra-virgin olive oil and fresh lemon juice (never use bottled lemon juice!) with a dash of sea salt and freshly ground pepper. **TWO** Lay the salmon onto a chilled plate in a single layer. Arrange the sliced gherkins and lemon slices on top of the salmon. Dress the salmon with the vinaigrette and top with the arugula.

Serves 6

CARPACCIO MANIA Most diners are aware of the famous raw beef tenderloin carpaccio, known to have originated at *Harry's Bar* in Venice. We've taken the liberty to call just about anything laid out like a carpet a carpaccio including veal, beef, pork, salmon, tuna, swordfish, various salami, cured meats and even Portobello mushroom, pineapple and melon. If you can slice it thin, you can present it carpaccio style.

Rosticini

In Abruzzo they have special charcoal grills, four feet wide and only six inches deep, where they can lay out literally a hundred rosticini at a time. Usually made of lamb, rosticini are consumed by the dozens as snacks sold by street vendors. The skewers are prepared by packing the meat in a special metal box with slits in the sides of it to facilitate cutting. With this tool a hundred precisely carved rosticini can be produced in a matter of minutes. You can get comparable results by using a charcoal or gas grill and skewering the meat by hand.

INGREDIENTS *2 lbs boneless lamb* ‖ *½ cup extra-virgin olive oil* ‖ *2 tablespoons red wine vinegar* ‖ *1 teaspoon Worcestershire sauce* ‖ *½ cup onion, finely chopped* ‖ *½ cup carrot, finely chopped* ‖ *½ cup celery, finely chopped* ‖ *2 cloves garlic, finely chopped* ‖ *1 sprig fresh rosemary, stripped from stem and chopped* ‖ *2 bay leaves, crumbled by hand* ‖ *To taste, Kosher salt and freshly ground pepper* ‖ *As needed, wooden or metal skewers*

ONE Soak the wooden skewers in water at least two hours or overnight (wet skewers tend not to burn). Trim the excess fat and cut the meat into small cubes. **TWO** Thread the meat onto the skewers until you use up all of the meat. The amount of rosticini you have will vary depending upon the size of the cubes. **THREE** Combine the remaining ingredients into a bowl and mix well to make a marinade. Cover the rosticini in the marinade for at least one hour for better cuts of meat or for as long as overnight for lower grades of meat. The vinegar and oil in the marinade will help to tenderize the meat. **FOUR** Pre-heat the grill, with the cover on, for 15-20 minutes. Place the rosticini on the grill and cook for 5-10 minutes or until the meat is done. Season with a generous amount of Kosher salt before serving.

Serves 6

ROSTICINI MANIA You can still use your backyard grill but you'll eventually want to get a *spiedini* box if you really want the authentic Italian rosticini experience. The ones we use at *Mario's* are ordered from www.fabermec.it. The illustrations on the box show you how you can use this unique device to make kabobs out of any kind of meat, fish, fruit, or even skewered sandwich kabobs!

Bresaola with arugula and parmigiano-reggiano

Bresaola is air-cured lean beef, usually top or bottom round, aged with salt and spices. It's classic Italian charcuterie that has a deep beefy flavor and a musty aroma quite unlike anything else. Here it is sliced paper thin and laid out on a plate carpaccio style, as is the custom in many Italian restaurants. It's dressed with lemon juice, extra-virgin olive oil and freshly ground pepper. Shaved grana-padana or parmigiano-reggiano cheese and fresh arugula finish the presentation. This dish is simple, classic, authentic Italian food at its best.

INGREDIENTS *8 oz bresaola, very thinly sliced* ‖ *2 lemons, cut into wedges* ‖ *½ cup extra-virgin olive oil* ‖ *2 bunches arugula* ‖ *2 oz parmigiano-reggiano or grana-padana cheese, shaved* ‖ *To taste, freshly ground black pepper*

ONE Arrange the bresaola on a plate and dress with a drizzle of extra-virgin olive oil and freshly ground black pepper. Top with arugula and shaved cheese. Serve with a wedge or two of fresh lemon.

Serves 6

THE BUSIEST DAYS AT MARIO'S New Year's Eve and Valentine's Day are the two busiest nights of the year for most restaurants. For us that means feeding 3-4 times more customers than we would normally plus the bar gets raised even higher because the demand for more difficult to execute upscale cuisine, as opposed to dishes like spaghetti and meatballs, also increases. This was a ticket to disaster for us on first couple of these special occasion days before we decided, many years ago now, to go with a prix-fixe, i.e. fixed price menu. What that means is we offer a set menu, in this case a five-course menu, and a set price. Each person chooses one of four options for each course. The prix-fixe menu has been well received by our customers, although we still accommodate the occasional request for that spaghetti and meatballs! This bresaola, like many of the recipes in this book, was developed for one of these special occasion menus. Like many others that first appeared on a prix-fixe menu, bresaola also made an appearance on the regular menu.

Coppa and cucumber carpaccio

A variation on the carpaccio theme, this dish has been featured with great success as a Sunday brunch antipasto, and on special occasion menus. People have absolutely loved this dish when it has been presented to them as the flavors just explode in your mouth. We trust that you will enjoy it as well.

INGREDIENTS *8 oz coppa salami, sweet or hot, very thinly sliced* ‖ *2-3 medium sized cucumbers, very thinly sliced lengthwise using mandoline, or crosswise using a knife* ‖ *2 ounces parmigiano-reggiano or grana-padana cheese, shaved* ‖ *3 oz arugula* ‖ *⅓ cup extra-virgin olive oil* ‖ *⅔ cup white wine or champagne vinegar* ‖ *2 tablespoons chives, chopped* ‖ *To taste, Kosher salt and freshly ground pepper*

ONE Place a single layer of salami onto a chilled plate. Scatter the arugula and shaved cheese on top of the salami to create a second layer. Layer the cucumber slices on top of the arugula and top with the shaved cheese. **TWO** Make champagne vinaigrette by whisking together the olive oil, chives, vinegar, Kosher salt, and freshly ground pepper to taste. **THREE** Dress the carpaccio with the vinaigrette just prior to serving.

Serves 6

WHAT'S A MANDOLINE? You might have seen one of these popular culinary tools being hawked on late night TV. A mandoline is basically a flat surface with a blade in the middle of it. You can pass vegetables, tomatoes, cucumbers, carrots, etc. over the blade to get slices and julienne cuts. Although the term mandoline wasn't used until sometime in the mid 20th century, the earliest known cooking mandoline is depicted in an Italian cookbook dating back to 1570. Chalk another one up to Italian ingenuity.

Bruschetta al pomodoro Traditional bruschetta are grilled slices of rustic bread, rubbed with whole cloves of fresh garlic and drizzled with extra-virgin olive oil. Originally from Abruzzi, bruschetta are now topped with everything imaginable including of course fresh tomatoes as in this recipe.

INGREDIENTS *1 loaf rustic Italian style bread such as ciabatta or filone ‖ 2 lb ripe tomatoes ‖ ½ teaspoon garlic, chopped ‖ 1 cup arugula, roughly chopped ‖ ½ cup extra-virgin olive oil ‖ 2 tablespoons white balsamic vinegar ‖ To taste, Kosher salt and freshly ground black pepper ‖ 3 oz parmigiano-reggiano or grana-padana, shaved or grated*

ONE Using a paring knife, cut a small x in the top of the tomatoes. Submerge them in boiling water for about one minute or until the skins begin to blister. Remove and cool them down in ice water. Peel and cut in half. Gently squeeze out the seeds and chop. **TWO** Slice the bread. Drizzle a small amount of olive oil onto each slice and season to taste with salt and pepper. Grill on a hot char-broiler or toast under broiler. **THREE** Top each slice with the tomato mixture. Garnish with shaved cheese and additional arugula and serve promptly before the bread becomes soggy from the tomatoes.

Serves 6

BRUSCHETTA MANIA! An interesting and fun way to do bruschetta is to prepare several different toppings using different ingredients. Some examples are mushrooms, artichokes, olives, beans, and cheeses. Two or three different brushetta can be lined up on a platter or the different toppings can be presented in bowls so your guests can customize their own.

Crazy bread

This is garlic-bread on steroids. We had this on the menu during our *Mario's Italian Steakhouse* years. This bread is loaded with cheeses, mayonnaise and our signature garlic butter.

INGREDIENTS *1 loaf your favorite Italian bread, such as ciabatta or filone ‖ ½ cup garlic butter (see page 14) ‖ ½ cup mayonnaise ‖ ¼ cup extra-virgin olive oil ‖ 3 oz mozzarella, shredded ‖ 1 ounce Asiago cheese, shredded ‖ 1 oz gorgonzola, crumbled ‖ 1 oz dry ricotta cheese, cut into small cubes ‖ To taste, Kosher salt and freshly ground pepper*

ONE Cut the bread in half lengthwise down the middle so that you have a top half and a bottom half. **TWO** Drizzle olive oil across the open face of the bread and season with Kosher salt and freshly ground black pepper. Grill the bread face down on a pre-heated char-broiler or otherwise toast under the broiler setting of your oven. **THREE** Generously spread garlic butter across the length of the bread slices. Spread a layer of mayonnaise over the butter. Combine the mozzarella, asiago, gorgonzola, and dry ricotta cheeses and spread them out evenly over the face of the bread. **FOUR** Place the bread on a suitably sized baking pan. Bake in a pre-heated 350° F oven for 6-8 minutes or until the cheese is melted and bubbly. Slice and serve with optional grated cheese.

Serves 6

THIS BREAD IS KILLER! The prototype for this recipe originated at *Mario's Pizza & Pasta* on East Avenue. The story goes that one of the employees loved it and made the remark "This bread is killer!" (For those who missed the eighties, to say something was "killer" meant it was great or awesome.) The name stuck and thus it came to be called Killer Bread. The recipe has changed somewhat and we changed the name to Crazy Bread, but the basic idea of heavily lacing traditional garlic bread with mayonnaise and several types of cheese remains the same.

Roasted portobello mushroom with rosemary-gorgonzola butter

Because of their size, Portobello mushrooms lend themselves to a variety of presentations that other mushrooms simply cannot measure up to. A more finger friendly alternative would be to use smaller "baby bellas" or Italian brown crimini mushrooms.

INGREDIENTS *6 large Portobello mushroom caps* ‖ *½ cup extra-virgin olive oil* ‖ *½ lb butter, unsalted* ‖ *¼ lb gorgonzola cheese* ‖ *2 tablespoon rosemary, stripped from the stem and chopped* ‖ *1 tablespoon parsley, chopped* ‖ *1 teaspoon thyme, stripped from the stem and chopped* ‖ *2 tablespoon shallots, chopped fine* ‖ *To taste, Kosher salt and freshly ground pepper*

ONE Place the butter, gorgonzola, and shallots into a mixing bowl and whip on high speed for four minutes. Add the herbs, season with salt and pepper and continue mixing for another minute or until the butter becomes light and airy. **TWO** Brush or carefully rinse any visible debris from the mushrooms and season them to taste with salt and pepper. Drizzle with a small amount of olive oil. Place them onto a large baking pan and roast in a preheated 350° F oven for about 5 minutes or until the mushroom is *just* cooked. Remove the caps from the oven and place a dollop of the butter onto each. Place them back into the oven until the butter begins to melt and serve while the butter is still foamy.

Serves 6

MUSHROOM TRIVIA Have you ever noticed that Portobello mushrooms look like larger, opened-up crimini or Italian brown mushrooms? That's because they are the same mushroom, only fully mature. Did you ever notice how crimini, baby bellas and brown mushrooms look about the same as the common button mushroom only darker? That's because they are the same mushroom only from a darker strain. All of these mushrooms are the same species: *agaricus bisporus*.

Zucchini & ricotta involtini

This take on a classic vegetable rolls, or *involtini,* first appeared as an appetizer on our menu in 1990. For best results, slice the zucchini very thin on a mandoline and use high-quality fresh ricotta. The best ricotta will cling together better and be more flavorful than typical supermarket ricotta, which tends to be bland and very loose in texture.

INGREDIENTS *3 zucchini squash, thinly sliced lengthwise* ‖ *4 cups ricotta cheese* ‖ *2 lemons, zested and juiced* ‖ *½ cup extra-virgin olive oil* ‖ *2 good pinches crushed red pepper flakes* ‖ *To taste, Kosher salt freshly ground black pepper* ‖ *2 oz micro-greens, for garnish* ‖ *½ cup extra-virgin olive oil mixed with ¼ teaspoon Hungarian paprika and ¼ teaspoon cayenne pepper (optional garnish)*

ONE Using a mandoline, cut the zucchini into thin strips. Brush the slices using the remaining olive oil and season to taste with Kosher salt and freshly cracked black pepper. Grill the zucchini over high heat for about 1 minute per side or until *just* cooked. Set aside to cool to room temperature. **TWO** Chop up the lemon zest. Combine the ricotta with the lemon zest, half of the olive oil, and the red pepper flakes in a mixing bowl. Season to taste with freshly ground pepper and Kosher salt and mix to combine. Roll up the squash with a dollop of the ricotta mixture. **THREE** Heat the oil, paprika and cayenne mixture over medium heat for several minutes to allow the spices to infuse into the oil. Remove from the heat and set aside to cool. **FOUR** Dress the plates with a drizzle of the infused oil. Place the zucchini rolls onto a serving plate, cheese side down and garnish with the micro-greens on top.

Serves 6

STUZZICHINI This makes a great antipasti course by itself or as one of several "little bites" or *stuzzichini.* You can prepare *stuzzichini* on a mixed antipasto plate, perhaps accompanied by the *bruschetta al pomodoro* and *shrimp with pancetta and arugula* from this book.

Portobello mille foglie with warm charred tomato vinaigrette

In Italy, the descriptive term for multi-layered dishes is *mille foglie,* similar to the way the term *Napoleon* is used in French cuisine. For better stacking, try to pick out eggplant and tomatoes that will yield the same diameter slices as the Portobello. You can serve one of these as an antipasti course or two as a vegetarian entrée.

INGREDIENTS *6 large portobello mushroom caps ‖ 1 large eggplant ‖ 2 medium red onion ‖ 2 (9 oz) bags fresh spinach ‖ 12 oz fresh mozzarella, sliced ¼ inch thick ‖ 2 large ripe tomatoes ‖ ⅓ cup extra-virgin olive oil ‖ To taste, Kosher salt and freshly ground black pepper ‖ As needed, cleaned baby spinach (optional garnish)*

CHARRED TOMATO VINAIGRETTE *1½ lb plum tomato, cut into wedges ‖ 1 cup white onion, peeled and cut up ‖ ⅓ cup extra virgin oil ‖ ⅓ cup balsamic vinegar ‖ 6-8 cloves garlic ‖ ½ cup basil, packed ‖ To taste, Kosher salt and freshly ground black pepper*

ONE Peel the eggplant and onion and slice them together with the tomatoes into six ¾ inch slices. Brush the onions, tomatoes, eggplant, and mushrooms with oil and season to taste with salt and pepper. Grill the vegetables on a char-grill to obtain until they are cooked throughout. **TWO** Heat the olive oil in a large sauté pan over medium heat, add the spinach, and cook to wilt. Season to taste with salt and pepper. **THREE** Stack the vegetables, starting with the eggplant on the bottom followed by the spinach, tomato, onion, cheese and lastly the mushroom. Place the stacks on a sheet pan. **FOUR** For the tomato vinaigrette: Brush oil onto the onion, tomato, and garlic. Roast them on a baking pan in a pre-heated 400° F oven using the broiler setting, for 8-10 minutes to obtain a nice char. Transfer to a food processor or blender. Blend the vegetables together with fresh basil and balsamic vinegar until smooth. Season to taste with salt and pepper. Add the olive oil and blend briefly to incorporate. Serve warm. **FIVE** Turn the oven down to 350° F and place the Napoleon stacks in the oven to warm throughout and melt the cheese. Serve with the vinaigrette. The optional garnish is fried spinach leaves. To make the garnish fry fresh spinach in preheated 350° F oil.

Serves 6

CHARRING TOMATOES The concept of charring tomatoes is not particularly Italian. It is a technique usually associated with Mexico and the Americas, where charred tomatoes are frequently used to make salsa. We figured marrying this technique with basil and balsamic vinegar instead of cilantro and chilies would make this close enough to call it Italian Fusion cooking. Besides, it just flat out tastes good.

Arancini

These are breaded and fried risotto balls. We'll admit that it does take a bit of effort to make these, but it will be worth it when you cut into one of them and the rice and cheese oozes out like creamy risotto encased in a breadcrumb shell.

INGREDIENTS *1 lb Arborio rice ‖ ¼ cup extra-virgin olive oil ‖ 6 oz unsalted butter ‖ 1 cup onion, diced ‖ 1 cup carrots, peeled, diced and blanched ‖ 1 cup peas, fresh blanched or frozen ‖ 1 bay leaf ‖ 1 cup white wine ‖ 1 quart chicken broth (see page 61) or use canned broth ‖ 6 oz asiago cheese, shredded ‖ 6 oz parmigiano-reggiano or grana-padana cheese, grated ‖ ¼ cup chopped Italian flat leaf parsley ‖ ½ cup chopped fresh basil ‖ To taste, Kosher salt and freshly ground black pepper ‖ 10-12 fresh mozzarella, ciliegie (cherry) sized balls, or larger fresh mozzarella cut into small cubes ‖ 8 large eggs ‖ 2 cups all-purpose flour ‖ 4 cups plain or Japanese breadcrumbs ‖ Mario's marinara sauce (see page 2) or use 1 jar Mario's Pasta sauce*

ONE Heat the olive oil and 1 ounce of the butter in a large heavy-bottomed pot. Add the onion, carrots, garlic, and bay leaf. Sauté for 2-3 minutes to sweat and soften the onion. Add the rice and stir to coat the rice. Allow the rice to fry in the oil for 2-3 minutes, stirring occasionally. It will start to caramelize slightly, but do not let it burn. Add the white wine and stir into the rice and *then* add the water (or chicken broth). **TWO** Bring the rice to a boil and simmer over medium heat until it is done, adding additional liquid if needed. The rice will be done when it still has some bit to it but is not crunchy. **THREE** Season the rice to taste with salt and pepper and incorporate the remaining butter and about half of each the cheeses. Remove from the heat and spread the rice out in a thin layer on sheet pans as needed to facilitate cooling. Set into the refrigerator to chill, making sure to toss it occasionally so that it will cool down evenly. **FOUR** Combine the cold rice in a large bowl with the peas, parsley, basil and the remaining cheeses. **FIVE** Roll the rice mixture into 5-6 ounce balls and insert a mozzarella ball into the center of each. **SIX** Whisk the eggs. Season the flour with salt and pepper to taste. Bread the rice balls first rolling them flour, then dip them in the egg and finally coat them with breadcrumbs. The final weight should be 6-7 ounces. **SEVEN** Heat your tabletop deep fryer or wok, or set a pan of frying oil on the stove with a clip-on thermometer and bring the temperature up to 325-350° F. Carefully fry the rice balls for 1-2 minutes or to obtain a golden brown color. Place onto a sheet pan and bake in a pre-heated 350° F oven for an additional 8-10 minutes or until the cheese has melted in the center. Serve with Mario's sauce for dipping.

Makes 10-12 balls

LEFTOVER RISOTTO We've stuffed rice with all varieties of meats, cheeses, and vegetables, often as a way to use up leftover risotto. If you can put it in a risotto dish you can roll it into an arancini!

Artichokes French

Some foodies may scoff at the idea of including this recipe in our collection of 100 recipes. After all, doesn't every Italian restaurant in Rochester, New York have a French dish on the menu? All we know for sure is we serve thousands upon thousands of artichoke, chicken, and veal French dishes every year so there can be no doubt that this dish remains an enduring favorite. We suspect for those that love this dish, particularly those that have had limited success preparing it at home, this may be the *one* recipe we should have included. You can, of course, substitute pounded veal cutlets or chicken breast for the artichokes in this recipe but additional cooking time will be required.

INGREDIENTS *2 (13¾ oz) cans whole artichokes ‖ 1½ cup all-purpose flour ‖ 6 large eggs ‖ 2 tablespoons Italian parsley, chopped ‖ ¾ cup sherry wine ‖ 1 cup chicken or vegetable broth ‖ 3 tablespoons unsalted butter and 2 tablespoons flour, for the sauce ‖ 6 oz unsalted butter ‖ 3 fresh lemons, juiced ‖ ½ cup parmigiano-reggiano or grana-padana cheese, grated ‖ To taste, Kosher salt and white pepper*

ONE Whisk together the egg and parsley and season to taste with salt and pepper. Drain the artichokes. Dredge the artichoke in flour, shaking off the excess before dipping them into the egg mixture. **TWO** Heat the oil in a large sauté pan over medium-high heat. The oil should be about ¼ - ½ inches deep. Be sure the oil is hot before adding the artichokes or they will stick to the pan. **THREE** Carefully, place the artichokes in the hot oil. The egg batter should set immediately and begin to brown slightly. After 20-30 seconds turn them over and cook for another minute or so. Remove the artichokes from the pan and empty out the oil. **FOUR** For the sauce: Return the pan to the stove over medium heat. Melt two tablespoons of butter in the pan before adding 2 tablespoon of flour. Mix to combine and form a roux. Cook the roux for 5 minutes, stirring occasionally. Add the chicken broth and simmer for several minutes, stirring occasionally to allow the broth to thicken. Add the lemon juice and sherry wine. Bring to a simmer and whisk in the remaining butter to incorporate. Season to taste with salt and white pepper. **FIVE** Add the artichokes back into the pan and bring to a simmer, allowing the artichokes to heat throughout. Plate the artichokes and dress them with the sauce. Garnish with chopped parsley and grated cheese.

Serves 6

IS FRENCH ITALIAN? Not exactly, but it's not exactly French either. The origin of this dish cannot be pinned down precisely except to say that it was well established in New York City by the 1950's. Italian-Americans who opened restaurants in the Big Apple are thought to have created it in response to the demand for French food, which at the time was very trendy in New York. So-called *French* dishes are popular in New York, New Jersey, and surrounding areas and they have largely remained confined to this region.

Fried taleggio with raspberry sauce

Taleggio is widely regarded as one of the great cheeses of the world. Touted for its deep, complex and a truly unique flavor, this cow's milk cheese is strictly regulated and produced only in the Lombardy region of Northern Italy. At *Mario's* we bread and deep fry this great cheese and serve it accompanied with raspberry sauce. You may think it sounds like a glorified version of a the deep fried mozzarella sticks they serve at burger joints, but we think it's more like the best fried cheese thing you'll ever eat.

INGREDIENTS *1½ lb Taleggio cheese ‖ 1 cup all-purpose flour ‖ 2 cups panko (Japanese) breadcrumbs ‖ 6 large eggs ‖ 3 cups salad oil, for frying ‖ 1 (10 oz) package frozen raspberries*

ONE Defrost the raspberries and strain them. Retain the juices. Purée the berries in a food processor or blender. Add back some of the juice to obtain a sauce consistency. Strain the seeds out using cheesecloth or a tea strainer. If you prefer, you might want to sweeten the sauce with a touch of sugar. **TWO** Cut the cheese into 18 roughly equal-sized pieces. Whisk the eggs. Dredge each piece of cheese in flour, covering all sides, then dip into the egg wash before rolling the cheese in the breadcrumbs, coating all sides. It is important the cheese is completely coated with the breadcrumbs to keep the cheese from leaking out when it is fried. **THREE** Add canola oil to cover the bottom of a Teflon-coated skillet. The oil should be about ½ inch deep. Get the oil very hot before adding the breaded cheese. Place as many pieces of cheese as you can comfortably fit into the pan and fry on all sides to set the breading and obtain a golden color. This will take 2-3 minutes. Once the cheese has been fried it should be soft (but not runny) and warm throughout. **FOUR** Serve the fried cheese with the raspberry sauce for dipping.

Serves 6

THAT CHEESE STINKS! Admittedly Taleggio does give off a, some would say, strong aroma, particularly after frying. If you are averse to strong smelling intensely flavored cheeses then this cheese may not be to your liking. If that's the case we recommend you substitute the Taleggio with something tame like Brie.

Panzerotto with black truffle and saffron cream sauce

Chef Dino Alberto Paganelli, one of the Abruzzi region's top chefs, taught us this dish. Small squares of phyllo dough are layered into a muffin pan and then filled with black truffle and a mixture of egg, cream, mushroom, and cheese. Once baked, they are served on a bed of saffron cream sauce. Simple, yet so elegant. We have featured this at Chef tables and on special event menus. We recommend investing in a flexible muffin mould so you can easily remove the *panzerotto* without breaking them.

INGREDIENTS *1 (16 oz) box phyllo dough ‖ 1 cup shredded asiago or other aged Italian cheese ‖ 6 large eggs ‖ ½ cup cream ‖ 6 crimini mushrooms ‖ 2-3 oz black truffle salsa ‖ To taste, Kosher salt and freshly ground black pepper*

SAFFRON CREAM SAUCE *4 cups heavy (whipping) cream ‖ A good pinch of saffron threads ‖ 1 tablespoon parmigiano-reggiano or grana-padana cheese, grated ‖ To taste, Kosher salt and white pepper*

ONE Defrost the phyllo. Carefully unroll and lay it out. Leaving the sheets stacked, cut about 10 sheets into six roughly equal sized square shapes. Stack the squares and cover with a damp cloth to keep them from drying out while you are working with them. **TWO** Whisk the egg and cream together and season the mixture to taste with salt and pepper. Slice the crimini mushrooms, as thinly as possible. Add the cheese and mushrooms to egg mixture and combine. **THREE** Spray the muffin pan with non-stick spray. Place seven layers of phyllo into each of six muffin cups to form the panzerotto. Put a small dollop of black truffle salsa in the bottom before filling the phyllo basket with the egg mixture to the level of the pan. **FOUR** Bake the panzerotto in a pre-heated 350° F oven for 15 minutes or until the egg mixture is set. Use a toothpick to test for doneness. **FIVE** For the saffron cream sauce: Boil the cream together with the saffron in a large, heavy-bottomed or non-stick pan. Cook the cream down to about half of its original volume. The cream will take on a distinct shine as it reduces to its proper thickness. Do not let the cream scorch on the bottom. Transfer to a clean saucepan and whisk in the cheese. Season to taste with salt and white pepper. Serve the panzerotto on a pool of the sauce.

Makes 6 panzerotto

WORKING WITH PHYLLO First, be sure to defrost the dough slowly overnight in the refrigerator. Once you open it, carefully lay it out and be aware that it dries up in a matter of minutes. Once dry it becomes extremely brittle and unworkable. Keep a moist, but not wet, towel over it and work quickly to remove the layers so that you can cover it back up.

Zuppe e ensalate—
Soups and salads

Lauren and Michael Daniele in Castelnuovo, Italy 2004

Minestrone soup

Like lasagna and meatballs, customers expect to see some kind of minestrone on the menu when they go to an Italian restaurant. This recipe is the result of months of tweaking. We finally knew we got it right when we started adding cabbage and parsnips, ingredients used in Italian cooking since pre-Roman times. We got the idea to add these vegetables from a minestrone recipe we found in an Italian cookbook that was published in the 1800's.

INGREDIENTS *½ cup extra-virgin olive oil* ‖ *¼ cup fresh garlic, chopped* ‖ *4 oz pancetta, sliced thin and cut into small pieces* ‖ *1 cup onion, peeled and chopped* ‖ *1 cup carrots, peeled, split in half and chopped* ‖ *1 cup celery, chopped* ‖ *1 cup parsnips, peeled, split into quarters and diced* ‖ *1 cup zucchini, split into quarters and sliced* ‖ *1 cup yellow squash, split into quarters and sliced* ‖ *½ pound cabbage, chopped* ‖ *2 cups plum tomatoes, diced* ‖ *1 cup cannellini or great northern white beans* ‖ *1 cup garbanzo (ceci) beans* ‖ *1 cup red kidney beans* ‖ *2½-3 quarts homemade chicken broth (see page 61) or use canned broth* ‖ *1 jar Mario's Pasta Sauce* ‖ *¼ teaspoon dry oregano* ‖ *½ cup basil pesto* ‖ *8 ounces ditalini pasta, pre-cooked* ‖ *To taste, Kosher salt and freshly ground pepper*

ONE Wash and carefully cut the vegetables into uniform sized pieces. The squash, parsnips, and carrots should be halved or quartered, depending upon size, and then sliced. Half moons are okay as long as the squash are not much bigger than 1 inch in diameter. They should be cut no thicker than ¼ inch. The green beans should be cut 1 inch in length. **TWO** Cook the pasta in boiling salted water for 8-10 minutes or until *al dente*. **THREE** Heat the olive oil in a large heavy-bottomed pot over medium heat. Add the pancetta and cook for 5 minutes. Add the garlic and sauté 3-4 minutes or until the garlic softens. Do not brown or burn the garlic. **FOUR** Add chicken stock, onion, carrot, celery, cabbage, and green beans. Bring to a simmer and cook 10 minutes. **FIVE** Add marinara, parsnips, yellow squash, and zucchini. Cook 3 minutes. **SIX** Add the chickpeas, red kidney beans, tomatoes, pesto, dried oregano, and pasta. Simmer briefly to allow the flavors to develop and season to taste with salt and pepper.

Makes about 4 quarts

THE BIG SOUP In Italian *minestrone*, literally translated, means "big soup." Every Italian region has its own traditions when it comes to the big soup, although they nearly always contain some kind of bean and pasta, in addition to numerous vegetables. Traditional Abruzzese minestrone is sometimes called The Virtues, or *le virtu*, because the ingredients, which are numerous, symbolize the many virtues of Abruzzese women.

Tiberius soup with veal, pork, and farro

We did a "guest chef" dinner with Chef Dino Paganelli, Executive Chef and culinary instructor of *Abruzzo Cibus* culinary tours based in Abruzzi, Italy. This is one of the dishes he taught us. Here we have cubed veal and pork simmered in a rich broth together with farro. Spinach and egg are added *stracciatella* style at the last minute and the dish is finished with a drizzle of olive oil and grated grana-padana or parmigiano-reggiano. Toasted bread slices complete the presentation.

INGREDIENTS *1 lb pork chops, or pork loin ‖ 1 lb veal, loin or round ‖ 2 cups farro (spelt) ‖ 1 cup extra-virgin olive oil ‖ 1 (9 oz) bag fresh spinach, cleaned, trimmed and roughly chopped ‖ 12 large eggs ‖ ½ gallon water or a light broth made from veal, pork or beef bouillon ‖ To taste, Kosher salt and freshly ground pepper ‖ 12 slices toasted baguette bread, grated cheese and olive oil, to serve*

ONE Cook the farro in 3 quarts of boiling salted water for 15-20 minutes or until it is about halfway cooked. Drain and set aside. **TWO** Cut and cube the pork and veal into roughly ¼ inch uniform pieces. Heat the olive oil in a large pot over medium-high heat. Add the veal, pork, and onion. Sauté for 4-5 minutes, stirring occasionally, to allow the meat to sear and onions to soften. **THREE** Add 2 quarts water or broth and the cooked farro to the pot and simmer over low heat for 30 minutes, until the farro is completely cooked and the meats are tender. Add Kosher salt and white pepper to taste. **FOUR** Mix the eggs with a fork and drizzle them slowly into the hot soup through a coarse wire mesh or pasta strainer. The idea is to get the eggs to stream out and look like "little rags" or *stracchiatelle.* Add the spinach. Serve with a drizzle of olive oil, some grated grana-padana or parmigiano-reggiano cheese and toasted or grilled bread.

Makes about 3 quarts

WHY IS IT CALLED TIBERIUS? Tiberius was one of Rome's greatest generals and emperor in the 1ˢᵗ century. Chef Dino Paganelli says it's named after him because this recipe is reminiscent of the ancient Roman dishes they prepared two thousand years ago. Farro, also known as spelt, is a form of wheat that was an important food grain in some parts of Europe, including Italy, from the Bronze Age to medieval times.

Spicy baby octopus and sweet pepper soup

This was our Abruzzese alternative to the American clam chowder that so many American-Italian restaurants are obligated to serve on Friday nights. Hot banana peppers give this soup a little zing, which is very common in the Abruzzi region where fresh and dried hot peppers are an important part of the local cuisine. When preparing this recipe, use baby octopi which are much more tender and easier to work with than the adult variety.

INGREDIENTS *4 lb baby octopus, fresh or frozen* ‖ *2 quarts water* ‖ *2 red bell peppers, cut into short thin strips* ‖ *2 green bell peppers, cut into short strips* ‖ *2 Spanish onions, peeled and cut into short strips* ‖ *2 hot banana peppers, cut into short strips* ‖ *8 cloves garlic, sliced thinly* ‖ *2 tablespoons Italian flat leaf parsley, chopped* ‖ *½ cup extra-virgin olive oil* ‖ *To taste, sea salt and freshly ground pepper*

ONE Simmer the octopi in two quarts of water for about 20 minutes or until they are tender. Strain and reserve the liquid. Cut them in half, separating the body and tentacles. The larger ones may need to be cut in half again. **TWO** Sauté the onion and garlic in extra-virgin olive oil until the onion is soft. Add the cut octopi, along with half of the parsley, and sauté briefly. **THREE** Add the reserve liquid, sweet, and hot peppers and simmer for 20 minutes. Add the remaining parsley. The octopus broth should be naturally salty, but taste to see if it requires any additional salt or pepper.

Makes about 3 quarts

MARIO'S STAFF GOES TO ITALY Our staff was invited to partake in employee trips to Italy on two separate occasions (and there was also a California trip) in 1998 and then again in 2001. These were once-in-a-lifetime opportunities for all of us to tour Central Italy and study the cuisine and culture firsthand. The second of these trips in particular was a week long, hands-on culinary tour of the Abruzzi region under the auspices of the *William Schuman Foundation* as part of a cultural exchange program. We were able to get into the kitchens of one or two different restaurants per day (each day up at dawn and returning to our hotel sometime after midnight) to work and learn directly from the chefs. Many of the dishes we learned on these trips went on to become signature dishes for us at Mario's and are included in this book including this one which is this is the featured soup at the seafood restaurant *La Murena* in Pescara.

Scrippelle 'mbusse

This classic Italian soup from the Abruzzi region consists of delicate parmigiano-reggiano filled crepes in a light chicken broth. The broth gets ladled over the crepes at the last possible second before serving. In Abruzzi, this soup is often served at banquets and special occasions. It makes an elegant first course to any meal.

INGREDIENTS *8 cups homemade chicken broth, or used canned broth ‖ 12 crepes ‖ ½ cup parmigiano-reggiano, grana-padana cheese, grated ‖ 3 teaspoons chives, finely sliced*

HOMEMADE CHICKEN BROTH *1 whole chicken, cut up ‖ 1 cup onion, rough chopped ‖ 1 cup celery, rough chopped ‖ 1 cup carrot, rough chopped ‖ 8-10 whole black peppercorns ‖ 2 sprigs fresh parsley ‖ 1 sprig fresh thyme ‖ 1 bay leaf ‖ To taste, Kosher salt and white pepper*

CREPES *3 large eggs ‖ 1½ cups, all purpose flour, sifted then measured ‖ 1 cup milk ‖ ½ cup water ‖ 2 tablespoons melted butter ‖ 1 tablespoon, parsley ‖ 3 tablespoons parmigiano-reggiano cheese, grated ‖ 1 pinch, grated nutmeg*

ONE For the chicken broth: Place all of the ingredients into a stockpot and add water to cover. Bring to a boil over high heat. When it begins to boil a head of foam will develop which you should carefully remove. Simmer for 2 hours. Strain the stock carefully through a fine wire mesh strainer or folded cheesecloth and season with salt and white pepper to taste. **TWO** For the crepes: Put all the ingredients into a blender, food processor, or mixer and mix on high speed for one minute or until smooth. Refrigerate for 30 minutes. Heat a small non-stick omelet pan or crepe pan over med-high heat until the pan becomes hot. Add a small amount of butter to the pan to keep the batter from sticking. Ladle or spoon a small amount of the batter into the pan and tilt the pan to spread the batter into a thin layer about 4 inches in diameter. After the crepe begins to brown on the bottom carefully turn it over and continue cooking for about another 30 seconds until the crepe is nicely browned. Repeat until all of the batter is used up. **THREE** Lay the crepes out and sprinkle about half of the cheese onto them before either folding or rolling them up. Place two or three crepes into a serving bowl. Bring the broth to a boil and pour the hot stock over them at the last possible second before serving. Garnish with additional cheese.

Serves 6-8

CREPE MAKING We make fresh crepes for every Sunday brunch so we've had a lot of practice! The trick to making them is to be sure your non-stick pan is the right temperature before adding the crepe batter. This may take one or two trials to get it right but once the temperature is set you are good to go.

Lentils in beef broth

Lentils are grown in many regions of Italy, the most highly regarded of which are those harvested in the Abruzzi and Umbria regions of Central Italy. The Chefs at *Ristorante la Terrazza* in Sul Mare taught us how to prepare this traditional Abruzzese soup on one of our staff trips to Italy. This recipe calls for French brown lentils, which are widely available and similar to Italian lentils.

INGREDIENTS *1 lb French lentils ‖ 1 cup extra-virgin olive oil ‖ 8 oz prosciutto, roughly cut into 1 inch or so pieces, including rind ‖ 1 bay leaf ‖ 2 cups onions, diced ‖ 2 cups celery, diced ‖ 1 cup carrots, diced ‖ ½ gallon beef stock, homemade or made from beef base ‖ 4 cups potatoes, peeled and diced small ‖ To taste, Kosher salt and freshly ground pepper ‖ 1 (9 oz) bag cleaned fresh spinach, cut into strips*

ONE Carefully pick through the lentils to remove any stones or debris and rinse them in a colander with water. **TWO** Cook the diced potatoes in boiling water for several minutes until they are *just* done. Strain into a colander and set aside. **THREE** Heat up the oil over medium heat in a large thick-bottomed pot. Add the prosciutto rind and sauté in the oil for about 10 minutes to brown and render the fat. This is the most important step. **FOUR** Add the onions, celery, carrots, and bay leaf and sauté for 3 minutes to allow the vegetables to soften. **FIVE** Add the beef stock and lentils. Simmer for about 45 minutes or until the lentils are tender. Add the potato and spinach and simmer briefly to cook the spinach. Season to taste with Kosher salt and freshly ground pepper. Serve with freshly grated cheese and olive oil for drizzling.

Makes 3 quarts

A PROSCIUTTO POINTER Extracting the maximum flavor out of the prosciutto is the key to achieving authentic Italian taste in this recipe. Let the prosciutto cook 10 or more minutes slowly over medium heat until it begins to crisp like bacon. At this point, all the pork fat goodness has melted into the pan and the prosciutto, now browned, will add a caramelized element to the flavor profile.

Caprese salad with balsamic "caviar"

This is classic caprese salad taken to the next level with the addition of balsamic "caviar." Use only the best olive oil, the ripest heirloom tomatoes and imported Italian buffalo milk mozzarella, or *mozzarella di Bufala,* for this salad. We stumbled upon balsamic "caviar" while doing research for a holiday menu. It's a modern technique that is surprisingly easy to execute, the only special equipment you need is a plastic squeeze bottle and a wire strainer. Plus, you can tell your friends you have "gone molecular" with your gastronomy!

INGREDIENTS *2-3 heirloom tomatoes as needed, depending on size ‖ 3 (7-8 oz) mozzarella di Bufala ‖ ½ cup balsamic caviar, or substitute aged balsamic vinegar ‖ As needed, mixed frisée & arugula with sliced basil and radicchio, or any other delicate salad greens ‖ 1 cup extra-virgin olive oil ‖ To taste, Kosher salt and freshly ground black pepper*

BALSAMIC "CAVIAR" *3 fl oz balsamic vinegar ‖ 4 teaspoons plain gelatin powder ‖ 3 tablespoons cold water ‖ 1 quart olive oil*

ONE For the balsamic caviar: Put the olive oil in a wide-mouth container and place it in the freezer to chill. It should be as cold as possible while still remaining in a fluid state. **TWO** Mix four teaspoons plain gelatin with three tablespoons cold water. Set aside for 15 minutes to allow the gelatin to bloom. **THREE** Heat the balsamic vinegar to a simmer. Combine the gelatin with the vinegar and transfer the mixture to a squeeze bottle. Allow the mixture to cool down to room temperature. **FOUR** Remove the oil from the freezer and mix it to evenly distribute the cold oil. Drip the balsamic mixture, one drop at a time into the cold oil. Upon contact with the oil, the balsamic drop will immediately form a small ball, and slowly fall to the bottom of the container. Once you have used up all the balsamic mixture, set the oil container into the refrigerator and allow the caviar to set for 10 minutes. Strain the caviar through a wire mesh strainer. These will keep at least a week under refrigeration. **FIVE** Cut the tomatoes and mozzarella and arrange them on a plate. Dress with olive oil and balsamic caviar and garnish with the frisée mix. Apply pepper and salt to taste.

Serves 6

HEIRLOOM TOMATOES These tomatoes, which have been getting a lot of attention lately by the culinary community, are actually very old tomato varieties (hence the name heirloom) that were displaced by the bright red, perfectly round varieties that were later developed by horticulturalists. Despite having great, often superior flavor, consumers rejected them because of their misshapen forms and off-colored appearance.

Mario's seafood salad

This seafood salad hails from the Aprutina Coast. Here, the shellfish are lightly poached and combined with olives, roasted peppers, and capers. Good quality olive oil, fresh squeezed lemon juice, and a judicious use of sea salt are essential.

INGREDIENTS *1 lb fresh or frozen calamari, tubes and tentacles ‖ 1½ lb mussels ‖ 8 oz raw shrimp ‖ 8 oz sea scallops ‖ 5 lemons, cut in half ‖ ⅓ cup capers ‖ ⅔ cup green olives, sliced ‖ ⅔ cup, roasted red peppers, julienne cut ‖ ⅔ cup extra-virgin olive oil ‖ 2 teaspoons chopped parsley ‖ To taste, Kosher salt and freshly ground black pepper*

ONE Clean the squid, if not already cleaned. Pull and discard the long strand from the tentacle cluster, remove the quill and any membranes from the inside of the tubes and rinse. Slice the tubes into rings. **TWO** Place the mussels in a large sauté pan. Add 1 cup of water to the pan and cover. Steam the mussels over medium heat until they open. Drain the water from the mussels and set them in the refrigerator to cool. Once they are cool enough to handle, pick the mussels from their shells. Discard the empty shells and any arc unopened or have an off odor. **THREE** Bring 3 quarts of water to a simmer in a large pot. Squeeze the juice of 1 lemon into the water and drop the rinds into the pot with 3 tablespoons sea salt. Add the shrimp and scallops to the poaching water and cook for about 2 minutes before adding the squid. Continue to poach until all the seafood is *just* done, having turned from translucent to opaque. Carefully drain and refrigerate to cool. **FOUR** Once the shellfish has chilled, peel and devein the shrimp. Combine the shellfish with the olives, capers, roasted red peppers, and chopped parsley. Dress with extra-virgin olive oil and the juice from the remaining lemons. Season to taste with salt and pepper. Toss to combine and served with additional fresh lemon wedges.

Serves 6

WHY WE SALT THE WATER? Shrimp and other shellfish that come from the ocean have a naturally high salt content. Poaching them in unsalted water draws out that natural salt, resulting in a less flavorful final product. Ideally, you need to add enough salt to the water to achieve equilibrium between the salt in the water and the salt in the seafood. This means the poaching liquid should taste distinctly salty. A good rule of thumb is 1 tablespoon of salt per quart water. The seafood will not absorb the salt in the water and the natural salt will be retained.

Pear, walnut, and gorgonzola salad

Mario's son Danny came up with this clever take on a classic salad. Far from being an ordinary salad, this dish uses chopped radicchio and Belgian endive as a base and aged balsamic vinegar and honey as a dressing. Chopped pears, gorgonzola, and glazed walnuts complete the dish. Feel free to experiment with different types of honey.

INGREDIENTS *2 heads radicchio* ‖ *4 heads Belgian endive* ‖ *¾ cup crumbled gorgonzola cheese* ‖ *2 pears, Bosc or pear variety of your choice* ‖ *¾ cup glazed walnuts* ‖ *¾ cup aged balsamic vinegar* ‖ *¾ cup honey, any variety* ‖ *12 fresh chive sticks (optional for garnish)*

ONE Cut the radicchio and Belgian endive heads in half and remove the cores before chopping them into small, about ½ inch, cuts. Core and chop the pears into small sized cubes. **TWO** Place the cut radicchio and Belgian endive onto six chilled plates. Dress each salad by drizzling the honey and balsamic vinegar over each. Top with chopped pears, glazed walnuts, and gorgonzola. Garnish with two crisscrossed chive sticks (optional).

Serves 6

DANNY DANIELE The youngest son of Mario and Flora Daniele, Danny has in many ways become the driving force behind much of the family business. It was Danny who spearheaded our other restaurant projects *Bazil-A Casual Italian Kitchen* and *The Original Crab Shack*. Danny and his wife, April, live in Pittsford with their children, Caleb and Grace. The Veal Pazzo recipe *(see page 144)* is another of Danny's creations.

Grilled Caesar salad

At *Mario's*, we split a head of romaine lettuce and mark it on the char-grill for a couple of minutes before assembling our Caesar salad, an atypical approach to the classic dish. Trust us, this method is extremely popular and gets nothing but compliments from our customers. Whether you choose to make the salad our way or toss it the traditional way, you'll need a good dressing and we highly recommend ours.

INGREDIENTS *3 large romaine lettuce hearts ‖ 1 pint cherry tomatoes, sliced ‖ 1 cup red onion, chopped fine ‖ 2-2½ cups Caesar salad dressing ‖ 12 slices Italian bread or baguette, for croutons ‖ 2 ounces grana-padana cheese, shaved ‖ ¾ cup extra-virgin olive oil ‖ To taste, Kosher salt and freshly ground pepper*

CAESAR DRESSING *1 cup extra virgin olive oil ‖ ½ cup salad oil ‖ 1 egg ‖ 2 tablespoons Dijon mustard ‖ 6-8 anchovies ‖ 1 tablespoon heavy (whipping) cream, optional ‖ 1 teaspoon Worcestershire sauce ‖ 1 teaspoon Tabasco sauce ‖ ⅓ cup fresh garlic cloves ‖ To taste, freshly ground pepper*

ONE Remove or trim away any brown or wilted leaves from the romaine. Split the romaine heads down the middle lengthwise. Drizzle olive oil onto the cut side of romaine and season to taste with salt and pepper. Place the romaine cut side down, onto a pre-heated char-grill. Grill the romaine for about 30-60 seconds to obtain nice grill marks. **TWO** To make croutons: Place the sliced Italian bread onto a sheet pan. Drizzle generously with the remaining olive oil. Season to taste with freshly ground pepper and Kosher salt and top with some of the cheese. Bake in a 350° F oven for 4-5 minutes to crisp up the bread and melt the cheese. **THREE** To make the Caesar dressing: Place the garlic and anchovies into a food processor or blender; pulse until they are well chopped. With the processor running, add the egg, mustard, red wine vinegar, Tabasco, and black pepper and blend for 1 full minute. Slowly add the oils by drizzling them in a thin stream into the mixture. This should take a full 2 minutes. Add the heavy cream and process an additional minute. **FOUR** Place the romaine onto individual plates and drizzle the dressing over the lettuce. Top the lettuce decoratively with the remaining cheese, tomatoes, red onions, and garnish with two croutons.

Serves 6

GRILLED LETTUCE? The idea of grilling a salad lettuce may at first seem like a bad idea, but it's not that different from eating grilled asparagus or another grilled vegetable. It's a great technique that you can use to create interesting salads, side dishes, and entrees. For example, try wrapping pancetta around a wedge of radicchio or Belgian endive and grilling it. Dress with a drizzle of good olive oil and balsamic vinegar. Fantastic!

Pretzellini

Arugula, roasted red onion and cured olive salad

Arugula, or in Italian *rucola,* is a leafy green that is relatively unknown to most American cooks. It has a unique peppery flavor that is assertive enough to use as a fresh herb but still mild enough to serve as a salad green. We love arugula at *Mario's* and have featured it in numerous dishes that have been on our menus over the years, several of them are in this book.

INGREDIENTS *2 bags (5 oz) arugula ‖ ⅓ cup aged balsamic vinegar ‖ ¾ cup extra-virgin olive oil ‖ 6 oz oil cured olives, pitted ‖ 6 ounces dry ricotta cheese (ricotta salada), cut into ¼ inch cubes or crumbled ‖ 2 medium red onions, peeled & sliced ½ inch thick ‖ To taste, Kosher salt and freshly ground pepper*

ONE Place the red onion slices onto a sheet pan, brush with extra-virgin olive oil, and season to taste with salt and pepper. Roast them in the oven at 350° F for 15-20 minutes or until they soften and begin to brown slightly. Set aside to cool. **TWO** Place the arugula in a large bowl, add the balsamic vinegar and olive oil. Season to taste with salt and pepper and toss gently. **THREE** Add the red onions, oil cured olives, and about half the dry ricotta cheese to the bowl and toss it to coat with the residual dressing. If needed, add additional vinegar and oil to lightly coat the ingredients. **FOUR** Place the salad onto a plate and garnish with the remaining cheese. Garnish with two *Mario's* pretzellini (optional).

Serves 6

MARIO'S PRETZELLINI Mario's son Danny had wanted something to put on the tables that would serve as an edible centerpiece for quite some time until one day, upon seeing fried linguine being used as a garnish for a salad, it hit him. He knew he had found the perfect tabletop touch. They would later be dubbed *pretzellini* and are now being sold along with our sauces at grocery stores throughout the Northeastern United States.

Primi—
Pasta and risotto

Mario Daniele, age 6; Mario, age 18; Mario, age 20

Homemade fresh pasta

We believe that semolina is the secret to making great pasta at home. Semolina is a type of flour made from the heart of the wheat grain, where it is hardest, resulting in a firm pasta with a decent bite to it. You just don't get that same bite with ordinary flour. We use a 1:1 ratio of all-purpose flour to semolina when we make strand pasta like fettuccine and spaghetti and a 7:1 ratio for the pasta sheets we use for ravioli and lasagna where, a softer dough is preferred. It takes a bit more elbow grease to make fresh pasta with semolina, but the resulting pasta is much more satisfying and well worth the extra effort. Anyone willing to invest in a Kitchen-Aid or hand-cranked, counter-top mounted pasta maker can craft great pasta. These tools come standard with a fettuccine and spaghetti cutter, as well as a sheet roller for making pasta sheets.

INGREDIENTS *2 cups durum wheat semolina (or ½ cup semolina flour for ravioli or lasagna) ‖ 2 cups all-purpose flour (or 3½ cups for ravioli or lasagna), sifted then measured ‖ 4 whole large eggs ‖ 2½-3 fl oz water*

ONE Mix the semolina and all-purpose flour together. Form a well in the center of the flour and add the eggs. Work the eggs into the flour using a fork. Add 2½ ounces of water and continue to incorporate the wet ingredients into the dry, using your hands once the dough becomes unmanageable with a fork, until the flour has absorbed all of the liquid. The absorption of liquid will depend on the moisture in the flour, which can vary, so additional water may be required. Ideally add less, rather than more liquid. Alternatively, use a heavy-duty mixer; such as a Kitchen-Aid with dough hook attachment. **TWO** Cut off a portion of the dough and run it through a pasta sheeter using the thickest possible setting. Fold the dough and run it through the sheeter several times, folding it each time, until the dough achieves a uniform color and smooth texture. At this point, adjust the sheeter setting to the desired final thickness for the last pass through the sheeter. As each sheet is prepared, be sure to cover it with plastic wrap to avoid drying it out. **THREE** For fettuccine or spaghetti: dust each sheet with semolina or all-purpose flour and run through the pasta cutter. The semolina will prevent the pasta from sticking. Keep well wrapped until use. It is best to store in the freezer if you do not intend to cook it right away.

Makes 2 pounds 3 ounces

THANKS TONY! On Saturday nights two strolling musicians entertain in the dining room at *Mario's* by singing classic Old World Italian ballads and playing tunes on the accordion with guitar accompaniment. The dazzlingly talented gentleman who plays accordion is Tony Bozza. He also makes our homemade fresh pasta, including the fresh sheets we use to make lasagna and ravioli. We are honored to pass his pasta-making secrets on to you.

Lasagne *al forno*

Although it has evolved and changed somewhat over the years, *Mario's* has always had lasagna on the menu. This evolution ultimately represents what our customers have asked for which is good old-fashioned Italian-American lasagna, thick and cheesy with alternating layers of meat and ricotta cheese.

INGREDIENTS *1½ lb ground beef ‖ ¾ lb ground pork ‖ ½ lb ground sausage ‖ 2 bay leaves ‖ 1 cup onion, chopped ‖ ½ cup garlic, chopped ‖ 2 tablespoons Italian parsley, chopped ‖ ½ cup chopped basil ‖ ¾ cup extra-virgin olive oil ‖ 1 cup shredded asiago cheese ‖ 3 lb good quality ricotta cheese ‖ 3 large eggs ‖ 2 tablespoons chopped parsley ‖ ½ teaspoon granulated garlic ‖ To taste, Kosher salt and freshly ground black pepper ‖ 1 batch homemade fresh pasta (see page 76) or use pre-made store bought pasta sheets or cooked dry lasagna sheets ‖ 4 oz parmigiano-reggiano or grana-padana cheese, grated ‖ 12 oz mozzarella cheese, shredded ‖ Mario's marinara (see page 2) or 2-3 jars Mario's Pasta Sauce*

ONE Prepare one batch of homemade fresh pasta sheets using a hand-cranked pasta maker or Kitchen-Aid attachment adjusted to a thin-to-medium setting. **TWO** For the meat layers: Heat a large skillet over high heat. Add the olive oil, onions, and garlic and cook, stirring constantly, until the onions are soft. Add the parsley and basil and cook for 1 minute to allow the flavors to develop. Remove the onion mixture and set aside. Add the meats to the skillet and cook over high heat to brown, breaking them down as they cook. Season the meat to taste with salt and pepper and transfer it to a colander to drain and cool. Transfer to a large mixing bowl and combine with the cooked onion mixture, the asiago cheese and 2 cups of the marinara. **THREE** For the cheese layers: In a large bowl, mix together the ricotta, egg, parsley, garlic, and grated cheese. Season to taste with salt and pepper. **FOUR** Set up a large pot of lightly salted boiling water. Set up another container with ice water. Cook the pasta sheets, a manageable few at a time, for about 30-40 seconds, or as needed. Transfer them to the ice water to cool. **FIVE** To assemble the lasagna: Spoon a thin layer of marinara sauce in the bottom of a 9-by-12 inch baking dish. Add the first layer of pasta. Spread about half of the meat mixture evenly over it. Cover the meat with another thin, even layer of sauce and a generous sprinkling of grated cheese. Add a second layer of pasta. Spread about half of the ricotta cheese mix evenly over it. Cover the ricotta cheese with another thin, even layer of sauce and top with about half of the mozzarella. Layers 3 and 4 are the same as the first two. The fifth layer of pasta will be the last layer which should be topped with a final thin, even layer of marinara sauce. **SIX** Cover the pan with plastic wrap and then aluminum foil. Bake in a preheated 325° F oven for about 30 minutes, or until it is heated through and the cheeses have melted. Uncover and top with additional cheese, return to the oven for an additional 3-4 minutes to melt the cheese. Serve with additional marinara.

Serves 6

Lasagne with two salmons

This lasagna was on our menu in 1995 when *Mario's Via Abruzzi* first opened. It's an elegant recipe and we can't resist bringing bring it back from time to time for a special event or on one of our holiday menus. The two salmons here, fresh salmon and smoked, are layered with fresh pasta, spinach and Pernod cream sauce.

INGREDIENTS *1 batch of homemade fresh pasta (see page 76) or use pre-made store bought pasta sheets or cooked dry lasagna ‖ 2 pounds salmon filet, thinly sliced ‖ 1 pound sliced smoked salmon ‖ ½ lb mozzarella cheese ‖ 4 oz asiago cheese, shredded ‖ 2 bags (9 oz) fresh spinach ‖ To taste, sea salt and freshly ground pepper ‖ 1 jar Mario's Pasta Sauce*

PERNOD CREAM SAUCE *1 quart whole milk ‖ 2 cups heavy cream ‖ ¼ lb butter, unsalted ‖ ⅔ cup all-purpose flour ‖ 1 cup Pernod (anise flavored liquor) ‖ 1 tablespoon sugar ‖ To taste, Kosher salt and white pepper*

ONE Prepare one batch of homemade pasta sheets using a hand-cranked pasta maker or Kitchen-Aid attachment adjusted to a thin-to-medium setting. **TWO** To make the Pernod cream sauce: Melt the butter in a suitably sized sauté pan and mix the flour into the butter to form a roux. Cook the roux over low heat for 10-12 minutes, stirring regularly. In a separate pot, combine the milk, cream, and bring to a boil. Add the roux to the cream and simmer over low heat for 20 minutes. Add the Pernod and sugar, and simmer briefly before straining through a wire mesh strainer or cheesecloth. Season to taste with salt and white pepper. **THREE** Set up a large pot of lightly salted boiling water. Set up another container with ice water. Cook the pasta sheets, a manageable few at a time, for about 30-40 seconds, or as needed. Transfer them to the ice water bath to cool. **FOUR** Blanch the spinach in the pasta water by immersing it in the boiling pasta water and removing it immediately. Squeeze out the excess water. Lightly oil the spinach with olive oil and season to taste with salt and pepper. **FIVE** To assemble the lasagna: Dab a small amount of sauce on the bottom of a 9-by-12 inch casserole dish. Add the first layer of pasta and another thin, even layer of sauce. Add a single thin layer of fresh salmon and finally a layer of spinach. Ladle a small amount of sauce over the spinach and top with some of the mozzarella and asiago cheese. Repeat this procedure with the second layer using smoked salmon instead of fresh. The third and fourth layers will be identical to the first two. The fifth layer of pasta will be your last layer. Cover this last layer with more sauce. **SIX** Cover the lasagna with plastic wrap and then aluminum foil. Bake at 325° F for 30 minutes or until the salmon is cooked and the cheeses are melted. Remove the foil and plastic, sprinkle on additional grated cheese, and bake for 5 additional minutes to melt the cheese. Serve with marinara.

Serves 6-8

LASAGNE IS A SHAPE OF PASTA By definition; lasagne is a shape of pasta, not a specific pasta dish. Like any other form of pasta, there are countless ways this noodle can be prepared.

Cannelloni

These ground meat, ricotta, and spinach-filled pasta tubes were featured on the menu for several years at *Mario's*. This recipe is less ambitious to pull off than it looks. Purchasing pre-made pasta sheets will save time and simplify the preparation.

INGREDIENTS *1 batch homemade fresh pasta (see page 76), or use pre-made store bought pasta sheets ‖ 1 quart Alfredo sauce (see page 2) ‖ 1 lb ground beef ‖ 1 lb mixed ground veal and pork ‖ ½ lb boiled ham ‖ 1½ cup red onion, chopped ‖ 2 bags (9 oz) fresh spinach or frozen chopped spinach ‖ 2 lb ricotta cheese ‖ 1 cup parmigiano-reggiano or grana-padana cheese, grated ‖ 1 cup mozzarella cheese, shredded ‖ 4 large eggs ‖ 2 tablespoons butter, unsalted ‖ 1 oz fresh sage, stripped from the stem and chopped (or ¼ ounce dry rubbed sage) ‖ To taste, Kosher salt and freshly ground pepper*

ONE Prepare one batch of homemade fresh pasta sheets using a hand-cranked pasta maker or Kitchen Aid attachment adjusted to medium setting. **TWO** Cut the sheets into 5-inch widths to roughly form a square. Set up a large pot of lightly salted boiling water. Set up another container with ice water. Cook the pasta squares, a manageable few at a time, for about 30-40 seconds, or as needed. Transfer them to the ice water to cool. **THREE** Blanch the spinach in the pasta water by immersing it in the water and removing it immediately. Squeeze out the excess water once. If using frozen spinach, defrost and squeeze out the excess water. **FOUR** Using a food processor, separately process the ham, onion, and blanched spinach until they are finely chopped. **FIVE** Sauté the meats in a large skillet over high heat to brown, breaking them down as they cook. Add the sage and season to taste with salt and pepper. Transfer to a colander to drain and cool. Add butter to the skillet and sauté the ground ham and red onion until the onion is cooked. **SIX** Combine the ham and onion mixture, spinach, ricotta, eggs, and half the parmesan in a suitably sized bowl with the cooled meats. Season to taste with salt and pepper and mix well. **SEVEN** Roll the pasta squares up with about ½ cup of filling to form a cylinder. **EIGHT** Dab an even layer of Alfredo sauce in the bottom of a 9-by-12 inch baking dish. Place the cannelloni, seam side down, in a single layer in the dish. Cover with Alfredo sauce and top with the mozzarella cheese and the remaining grated cheese. Bake in a preheated 350° F oven for about 20 minutes, or until heated throughout and the cheese is melted and bubbly.

Serves 6

BROWNING MEATS In order to produce optimal flavor, ground meats need to brown as they cook. However, ground meats contain a great deal of water. As that water is released, the meat can end up stewing in its own juices rather than browning. To solve this problem, avoid overcrowding the pan, using a skillet with a large surface area. Be sure to cook over high heat to create faster water evaporation. Remember, you can't brown anything in water!

Whiskey scented ricotta cheese ravioli with spicy tomato-whiskey sauce

Sometimes a twist on something simple and direct is the best approach. The twist on this simple ricotta cheese filling is the addition of American whiskey (the sauce is also spiked with whiskey). These ravioli are better than good!

INGREDIENTS *1 batch homemade fresh pasta (see page 76)* ‖ *3 lb good quality ricotta cheese* ‖ *1 cup American whiskey* ‖ *¼ cup sugar* ‖ *3 large eggs* ‖ *To taste, Kosher salt and white pepper* ‖ *1 batch spicy tomato and whiskey sauce*

SPICY TOMATO AND WHISKEY SAUCE *2 (35 oz) cans whole peeled plum tomatoes* ‖ *1 can (10 oz) tomato paste* ‖ *1 cup American whiskey* ‖ *½ cup extra-virgin olive oil* ‖ *2 cup onions, chopped* ‖ *3 jalapeno peppers, chopped* ‖ *½ cup fresh basil, chopped* ‖ *1 teaspoon sugar* ‖ *To taste, Kosher salt and white pepper*

ONE Prepare one batch of homemade fresh pasta sheets using a hand-cranked pasta maker or Kitchen-Aid attachment adjusted to a thin setting. **TWO** For the filling: Combine the ricotta, sugar, whiskey, and eggs. Season to taste with salt and pepper. **THREE** For the spicy tomato and whiskey sauce: Heat the oil in a heavy-bottomed pot. Add the onion, basil, and jalapeno peppers and sauté until the onions are cooked. Break up the tomatoes with your hand and add them to the pot together with the tomato paste. Simmer over low heat for 15-20 minutes to develop the flavor. Process in a blender until smooth. Add the whiskey, sugar and to taste, salt and pepper and blend to combine. **FOUR** To prepare the ravioli: Hand-cut them or use a ravioli maker. Cut the sheets roughly 3 inches across so you will end up with 3-by-5 inch rectangles. Place a small amount of filling near the center of one rectangle, moisten the edges with water and fold the pasta over so that you have 3-by-2½ inch ravioli. Close the ravioli by pressing down on the open edges with a fork. If using a ravioli maker, lay the dough out onto the ravioli dye, fill the pockets, and cut according to the manufacturer's instructions. **FIVE** Bring a large pot of lightly salted water to boil over medium-high heat. Cook the ravioli for 5 minutes, or until the pasta is cooked and the filling is heated throughout. Serve with the whiskey sauce.

Serves 6

FREEZING RAVIOLI If you decide not to immediately serve your homemade ravioli, or you've found that you've made too much, you'll need to freeze them to prevent the filling from soaking through the pasta dough. Lay the ravioli out on a baking pan so they do not touch while they are freezing, or they will stick together and possibly break open when taking them apart. Once completely frozen they can be transferred to a zip lock bag.

Sea bass ravioli with tomatoes and baby clams

On our first staff trip to Italy we ate at *Ristorante Beccacecci*, a seafood restaurant in Giulianova. Among other outstanding offerings was a fish ravioli with clams dish that we were so enamored with that we decided to create our own version.

INGREDIENTS *1 batch homemade fresh pasta (see page 76) ‖ 2½ lb Chilean sea bass ‖ 6 cloves garlic ‖ 2 bay leaves, crushed ‖ ⅓ cup extra-virgin olive oil ‖ 1 cup dry white wine ‖ 5 egg whites, slightly beaten ‖ 1 cup panko (Japanese) breadcrumbs ‖ 1 tablespoon Italian parsley, chopped ‖ To taste, sea salt and freshly ground pepper*

TOMATO & CLAM SAUCE *4 lbs plum (Roma) tomatoes ‖ 3 dozen fresh or frozen cockle or baby clams ‖ 2 teaspoon garlic, chopped ‖ 1 cup extra-virgin olive oil ‖ 1 tablespoon Italian parsley, chopped ‖ To taste, Kosher salt and freshly ground black pepper*

ONE Prepare one batch of homemade fresh pasta. Prepare the pasta sheets using a hand-cranked pasta maker or Kitchen-Aid attachment adjusted to a thin setting. **TWO** For the filling: Place the fish in a roasting pan and season to taste with salt and pepper. Add the bay leaf, garlic, white wine and olive oil. Roast at 325° F for 20 minutes or until the fish is cooked throughout. At this point, you should be able to easily remove any bones. Remove the bay leaf and set the fish aside to cool. Break up the fish with your hands and transfer it to a food processor, reserving any of the cooking liquid left in the pan. Pulse for several seconds or until smooth. Transfer to a mixing bowl and add the egg white, breadcrumbs, and chopped parsley, along with some of the reserved liquid to moisten. **THREE** To make the ravioli: Hand-cut or use a ravioli maker. The standard sheeter that comes with a hand-cranked pasta maker is 5 inches wide. Cut the sheets roughly every 3 inches across so that you will end up with 3-by-5 inch rectangles. Place a small amount of filling near the center of one end of the rectangle, moisten the edges with water, and fold the pasta over so that you have 3-by-2½ inch ravioli. Close the ravioli by pressing down on the open edges with a fork. If using a ravioli maker, lay the dough out onto the ravioli die, fill the pockets, and cut according to the manufacturer's instructions. **FOUR** For the tomato-clam sauce: Use a paring knife to cut a small x in the top of the tomatoes. Submerge them in boiling water for about 1 minute or until the skins begin to blister. Remove and cool them in ice water. Peel and cut in half. Gently squeeze out the seeds and chop. Heat the olive oil in a skillet, add the garlic and cook 1 minute to slightly brown. Add the clams, parsley, and any remaining reserved pan liquid, cover and cook until the clams open up. Remove the clams from the pan and set aside. Add the tomatoes and cook until they are just done. Add the clams back to the pan and toss gently. Season to taste with salt and pepper. **FIVE** Cook the ravioli in boiling salted water for 3-5 minutes or until tender. Drain and serve with the tomato and clam sauce.

Serves 6

Beer battered fish-fry ravioli with creamy caper sauce

Yes-you read it right, this is fish-fry ravioli! A creation of Chef and ravioli master, James Dean. It may sound crazy but it's gotten nothing but rave reviews at table visits. When making these ravioli we fold them into triangles before crimping the edges, they look more like fried fish when prepared this way.

INGREDIENTS *1 batch homemade fresh pasta (see page 76)* ‖ *3 lb haddock* ‖ *¼ cup unsalted butter* ‖ *⅓ cup mayonnaise* ‖ *1 cup panko (Japanese) breadcrumbs* ‖ *4 large eggs* ‖ *1 lemon, juiced* ‖ *1 teaspoon Tabasco sauce* ‖ *1 dash Thai-style fish sauce (optional)* ‖ *To taste, sea salt and white pepper* ‖ *2 cans lager beer* ‖ *4 cups store bought fish & chips batter, plus 2 cups extra for dredging* ‖ *Oil, as needed for frying*

CAPER SAUCE *½ cup unsalted butter* ‖ *1 cup onion, diced* ‖ *½ cup all-purpose flour* ‖ *1 quart whole milk* ‖ *¼ cup capers* ‖ *¼ cup chopped dill pickles, plus ½ cup pickle juice* ‖ *1 teaspoon granulated garlic* ‖ *To taste, sea salt & white pepper*

COLESLAW *1 (16 oz) bag shredded cabbage for coleslaw mix* ‖ *1 head romaine lettuce, cut julienne* ‖ *1 head radicchio, cut julienne* ‖ *2 carrots, shredded* ‖ *12 fl oz pre-made coleslaw dressing* ‖ *¼ cup whole grain mustard* ‖ *To taste, cayenne pepper*

ONE Prepare one batch of homemade fresh pasta. Prepare pasta sheets using a hand-cranked pasta maker or Kitchen-Aid attachment adjusted to a medium setting. **TWO** For the filling: Place the haddock on a sheet pan or in a baking dish. Season to taste with white pepper and sea salt. Add ½ cup water and cover tightly with aluminum foil. Bake at 350° F for 10-15 minutes or until the fish is just cooked. Uncover and drain off the excess liquid. Refrigerate to cool. Combine the fish with the butter, mayonnaise, breadcrumbs, eggs, lemon juice, Tabasco and fish sauce into mixing bowl. Mix thoroughly and adjust seasoning to taste with salt and white pepper. **THREE** To make the ravioli: Cut the pasta sheets to get 5-by-5 inch pasta squares. Place a small amount of filling onto the pasta squares. Moisten the edges with water and fold over to get a triangle shape. Press down the edges with a fork. **FOUR** To make the batter: Whisk the beer into the dry batter mix. **FIVE** For the creamy caper sauce: Warm the butter in a saucepan and whisk in the flour to form a roux. Add the onion and cook over low heat for 8-10 minutes. Whisk in the milk and mix until smooth. Simmer over low heat for 20-30 minutes and strain through a wire mesh strainer. Add the remaining ingredients and simmer briefly to allow the flavor to develop. **SIX** For the coleslaw: Combine the shredded cabbage, romaine, radicchio, carrot, red onion, mustard, cayenne pepper and coleslaw dressing and mix to combine. **SEVEN** Par-cook the ravioli for 3 minutes in boiling water. Remove from the water and quickly dredge them in the remaining dry batter mix. Dip them into the wet batter and deep fry at 350° F for about 2 minutes per side, or until they turn golden brown. Serve the ravioli stacked on a pool of creamy caper sauce topped with coleslaw. Garnish with fresh lemon wedges.

Serves 6

Butternut squash tortoloni with apple-brandy cream sauce

We hand-make ravioli and tortoloni by the hundreds at *Mario's*. This is something we take pride in, especially considering most restaurants are more than happy to use pre-made product. In this recipe, which has become something of a seasonal specialty for us, we use local squash, apples, and cider. The fact that we never seem to be able to make these tortoloni quick enough says something about how good they are.

INGREDIENTS *1 batch homemade fresh pasta (see page 76)* ‖ *4 lb peeled and de-seeded butternut squash* ‖ *⅓ cup blackstrap molasses* ‖ *⅓ cup maple syrup* ‖ *⅓ cup sherry wine vinegar* ‖ *½ lb brown sugar* ‖ *½ teaspoon ground cinnamon* ‖ *½ teaspoon ground coriander* ‖ *½ teaspoon nutmeg* ‖ *½ teaspoon ground clove* ‖ *To taste, Kosher salt and white pepper* ‖ *½ lb asiago cheese, shredded* ‖ *6 cippolini onions, peeled* ‖ *2 apples, cored and sliced* ‖ *4 oz candied walnuts* ‖ *3 oz unsalted butter* ‖ *1 cup plain breadcrumbs, toasted*

APPLE-BRANDY CREAM SAUCE *8 cups heavy (whipping cream)* ‖ *2 cups brandy* ‖ *2 cups apple cider* ‖ *To taste, Kosher salt and white pepper*

ONE Prepare one batch of homemade fresh pasta sheets using a hand-cranked pasta maker or Kitchen-Aid attachment adjusted to a thin setting. **TWO** For the filling: Combine the molasses, maple syrup, sherry vinegar, brown sugar, cinnamon, coriander, nutmeg, and clove. Cut the squash as into chunks and toss to coat with the mixture to marinate. Transfer to a baking pan and roast at 325° F until the squash is tender. Remove the squash from the pan, taking care to leave behind any excess marinade, and process them until smooth. Season to taste with salt and white pepper. Add the cheese and combine. **THREE** For the tortoloni: Cut the resultant pasta sheets to obtain pasta squares. Place a small amount of filling onto each square, moisten the edges with water, and fold over to get a triangle shape. Wrap the triangle shapes around in a circle by connecting the opposite corners and fold over the middle corner to obtain a tortoloni shape. **FIVE** For the apple-brandy sauce: Combine the brandy and cider into a heavy-bottomed pot. Cook down by half over high heat. Add the heavy cream and cook down to obtain a sauce consistency. Season to taste with salt and white pepper. **SIX** Sauté the onions in minimal butter, over medium heat, until they are cooked throughout and well caramelized. Sauté the apples in butter over medium heat until they are soft and slightly caramelized. Toast the breadcrumbs in a 350° F oven for 10 minutes until golden brown. Add the onions and candied walnuts to the pan and sauté briefly. **SEVEN** Par-cook the ravioli for 5 minutes in boiling water or until the pasta is cooked and the filling is warm throughout. Toss with the sauce and garnish with the apples, walnuts, toasted breadcrumbs and onion.

Serves 6

THANKS JAMES! Chef James "Jimmy" Dean created this recipe, as well as the Beer Battered Fish-Fry Ravioli *(see page 88)* and Seafood Risotto recipes *(see page 124)*. James started his career with *Mario's* in 1999.

Scamorze cheese ravioli in saffron cream sauce

This ultra-rich ravioli dish was on our menu for a few years and we still feature it occasionally as one of our homemade ravioli specials. Scamorze is the quintessential Abruzzese cheese, mild with a distinctly nutty and slightly smoky flavor; these ravioli wouldn't taste the same with any other cheese. Fortunately, domestic scamorze is widely available.

INGREDIENTS *1 batch homemade fresh pasta (see page 76)* ‖ *1½ lb scamorze cheese, not smoked* ‖ *1½ lb good quality ricotta cheese* ‖ *5 egg whites* ‖ *1½ tablespoon Italian parsley, chopped* ‖ *To taste, Kosher salt and white pepper* ‖ *As needed, prosciutto, cut julienne and fresh basil leaf (optional garnish)*

SAFFRON CREAM SAUCE *8 cups heavy (whipping) cream* ‖ *1 tablespoon saffron threads* ‖ *1 cup parmigiano-reggiano or grana-padana cheese, grated* ‖ *To taste, Kosher salt and white pepper*

ONE Prepare one batch of homemade fresh pasta. Prepare the ravioli sheets using a hand-cranked pasta maker or Kitchen-Aid attachment adjusted to a thin setting. Carefully lay the sheets down, covering each layer with plastic wrap so they do not dry out. **TWO** Shred the scamorze cheese using a cheese grater. Combine the scamorze and ricotta into a food processor and blend. Add the egg white and parsley, and season to taste with salt and pepper. Blend to mix ingredients. **THREE** To make the ravioli: Hand-cut or use a ravioli maker. Cut the sheets roughly every three inches across so that you will end up with 3-by-5 inch rectangles. Place a small amount of filling near the center of one end of the rectangle. Moisten the edges with water and fold the pasta over so that you have 3-by-2½ inch ravioli. Close the ravioli by pressing down on the open edges with a fork. If using a ravioli maker, lay the dough out onto the ravioli die, fill the pockets, and cut according to the manufacturer's instructions. **FOUR** To make the saffron cream sauce: Bring the cream and saffron to a boil over high heat in an oversized heavy-bottomed pot. Cook the cream down to about half of its original volume. The cream will take on a distinct shine as it reduces to its proper thickness. Do not let the cream scorch on the bottom. Transfer to a clean saucepan and add the cheese. Season to taste with salt and white pepper. **FIVE** Boil the ravioli in salted water for 5 minutes, or until the pasta is cooked and the filling is heated throughout. Drain the ravioli and toss gently in the sauce. Serve garnished with a chiffonade of prosciutto, fresh basil leaves, and grated cheese.

Serves 6

RISTORANTE RIGOLETTO On our first staff trip to Italy we visited Sulmona, a tiny mountain village near Mario's hometown in the mountains of Abruzzi, where our friend Celestino Le Donne at *Ristorante Rigoletto* gave us the idea to develop this recipe.

Penne ortolano

This recipe was created at *Mario's* in 1996. The combination of tomatoes, garlic, artichokes, and spinach inspired the name *ortolano*, which means green grocer in Italian. It's the addition of capers, though, with their sprightly tang that really defines this dish. Capers are one of those fundamental Italian condiments that are irreplaceable in many classic Italian recipes. In the same way one can't imagine *puttanesca* sauce, chicken *piccata*, or eggplant *caponata* without capers, this dish simply wouldn't be the same without them.

INGREDIENTS *1½ lb penne pasta ‖ 2 lb plum tomatoes ‖ 1 can artichoke quarters, drained and rinsed ‖ 2 bag (9 oz) fresh spinach, stems removed ‖ 1½ cups extra virgin olive oil ‖ 4 cloves garlic, peeled and chopped ‖ 1 shallots, peeled and chopped ‖ 1 cup basil, chopped ‖ ½ cup capers ‖ 2 hot pepper pods or crushed red pepper (to taste) ‖ To taste, Kosher salt and freshly ground pepper*

ONE Use a paring knife to cut a small x in the top of the tomatoes. Submerge them in boiling water for about 1 minute or until the skins begin to blister. Remove and cool them in ice water. Peel and cut in half. Gently squeeze out the seeds and chop. **TWO** Blanch the spinach by submerging in boiling water for 1 second and then immersing in ice water to cool. Squeeze out the excess water. **THREE** Heat the oil in a large skillet over medium-high heat. Add the garlic and fry, stirring often, until the garlic becomes brown, but not burned. The garlic should be evenly colored and slightly darker than cardboard or cork. Add the shallots, hot pepper, and about half of the basil. Fry briefly until the shallots begin to soften. Add the tomatoes and continue to fry until the tomatoes are just cooked. Add the artichokes, spinach, capers, the remaining basil, and extra-virgin olive oil. Season to taste with salt and pepper. **FOUR** Cook the pasta in boiling salted water 8-10 minutes or until cooked to your preference. Drain the pasta and add it to the saucepan. Cook the pasta for 1 minute in the sauce to absorb the flavors and season as needed with salt and pepper. Add some of the pasta cooking water as needed to loosen if the dish becomes oily or dry. Serve with freshly grated cheese.

Serves 6

FAQ (NO. 1) "What is a caper?" Capers are the unopened flower bud of the caper plant, a shrub that grows wildly among the rocky hillsides throughout much of the Mediterranean. Used in sauces, stuffings, marinades, and salads, capers are most often associated with Sicilian cuisine. In the U.S., most capers are packed in jars with vinegar and sold as nonpareil capers, referring to their small size. In Italy and in some gourmet specialty shops, you can get them packed in salt, which is how Italian Chefs prefer them.

Fusilli *cavolfiore*

This would be a unique addition to anyone's pasta repertoire. Rarely do you see cauliflower, an under-appreciated winter vegetable, on a restaurant menu but after you've tried this dish you will find it hard to imagine a better vegetable to use. Here, the cauliflower is seared in the pan, where it picks up a nice brown color and caramelized flavor. Fusilli, spirelli, rotini, and other twisted pasta shapes are best to use with this dish because the ingredients tend to cling to the pasta better.

INGREDIENTS *1½ lb fusilli ‖ 1 head cauliflower, blanched and cut into small flat pieces ‖ 6 cloves garlic, chopped ‖ 4 oz pine nuts ‖ 4 oz raisins ‖ ½ cup extra-virgin olive oil ‖ 4 oz unsalted butter ‖ 4 oz breadcrumbs, Italian style ‖ 1 cup pasta cooking water or chicken stock*

ONE Cook the pasta in boiling salted water 8-10 minutes or until cooked to your preference. Drain the pasta and set aside. **TWO** Toast the breadcrumbs in a 350° F oven for 10 minutes until golden brown. **THREE** Heat the oil in a large skillet over high heat. Add the cauliflower and sauté to brown and slightly crisp it on the outside. **FOUR** Add the chopped garlic and raisins, cook until garlic is golden and raisins puff up. Add the cooked pasta and pasta water or chicken broth. Simmer over high heat until the liquid cooks down by half. Add the butter and season with salt and pepper. Garnish with toasted breadcrumbs.

Serves 6

ARE YOU READY FOR A PASTA THROW-DOWN? For several years running we've held a "Pasta Throw-Down" as part of the annual wine tasting event we hold in celebration of our wine list being given the Award for Excellence by the industry leading *Wine Spectator Magazine*. This pasta dish was entered by Chef Ron Olsheski the first year we had the throw-down. We didn't put out a ballot box and determine the winner, like we would go on to do in subsequent years, so we don't really know if this recipe would have won the throw-down or not, but we suspect it would have. Ronnie would officially emerge victorious in the throw-down a few years later. Ronnie went on to become the Executive Chef at *The Original Crab Shack*, our seafood restaurant.

Macaroni and cheese with applewood bacon and aged cheddar

This recipe was one of a quartet of mac-n-cheese dishes we had on the menu during the *Mario's Italian Steakhouse* days, all of which were available as either full entrées or side-dishes served alongside our steaks. For this recipe, we combine thick rigatoni pasta, aged white cheddar cheese, applewood smoked bacon, and fresh scallions with Mario's Alfredo sauce. Our creamy, garlicky, cheesy Alfredo is the perfect base sauce for macaroni & cheese.

INGREDIENTS *1½ lb rigatoni pasta ‖ 1 batch Mario's Alfredo sauce (see page 2) ‖ 1½ lb aged white cheddar (extra sharp or aged 1-2 years), shredded ‖ 18 strips applewood bacon ‖ 1 cup scallions, chopped ‖ 1 cup panko (Japanese) breadcrumbs*

ONE Prepare a batch of Mario's Alfredo sauce. **TWO** Lay the bacon out on a sheet pan and cook in a 350° F oven for 20 minutes or until it becomes crisp but not dry. Cut the bacon into ½ inch pieces. **THREE** Cook the pasta in boiling salted water about 10-12 minutes or until cooked to your preference. Drain the pasta, reserving a cup or so of the pasta water and transfer it to a suitably sized bowl. Season to taste with salt and pepper. Add the shredded cheddar and the scallions and toss to combine. **FOUR** Add 2 quarts of Alfredo sauce to the pasta mixture and toss to combine. The dish should be somewhat loose. Add reserved pasta water as needed. Transfer the mixture to a large 9-by-12 inch baking dish. Top with the remaining cheddar cheese and dust the top with the breadcrumbs. Bake in a 350° F oven for 10 minutes or until the cheese melts and begins to brown.

Serves 6

MACARONI AND CHEESE VARIATIONS We featured three other mac-n-cheese offerings on the Italian Steakhouse menu: black truffle & gruyere cheese, lobster macaroni-and-cheese, and a five cheese mac-n-cheese with gorgonzola, mozzarella, grana-padana, asiago, and aged provolone cheeses.

Fettuccine with asparagus, shiitake, and mascarpone cream sauce

In Italy, cream based pasta dishes are imbued with a certain lightness that is noticeably different from what most Americans are used to. A simple way to create a lighter sauce without sacrificing richness or depth of flavor is to use mascarpone, a fresh cream cheese, instead of butter to enrich the sauce. We learned this trick at *Ristorante La Tre Marie* in L'Aqulia, the capital of Abruzzi.

INGREDIENTS *1 batch homemade fresh pasta (see page 76) or use 2½ lb store bought fresh fettuccine ‖ 2 quarts heavy cream ‖ 1 cup mascarpone ‖ 1½ lb fresh asparagus ‖ 1 pound shiitake mushrooms, sliced ‖ 2 tablespoons shallot, peeled and chopped ‖ 12 fresh sage leaves, chopped ‖ ½ cup extra-virgin olive oil ‖ 3 tablespoons, parmigiano-reggiano or grana-padana cheese, grated ‖ To taste, Kosher salt and white pepper*

ONE Prepare one batch of homemade fresh pasta dough. Prepare the fettuccine using a hand-cranked pasta maker or Kitchen-Aid attachment or use store bought pre-made fresh fettuccine. **TWO** Bring the cream to a boil over high heat in an oversized, heavy-bottomed saucepan. Cook the cream down to about half of its original volume. The cream will take on a distinct shine as it reduces to its proper thickness. Do not let the cream scorch on the bottom. Transfer to a clean pan and whisk the mascarpone cheese into the cream to combine. Season to taste with salt and white pepper. **THREE** Blanch the asparagus in boiling water for 2 minutes or until it is *just* cooked. Cool down in ice water and cut on the bias into 2-3 inch lengths. **FOUR** In a large skillet, sauté the shallot in the olive oil for one minute over medium heat. Add the mushrooms and sage. Sauté until the mushrooms soften and season to taste with salt and white pepper. Add the mascarpone cream sauce, grated cheese, and asparagus and toss to combine. **FIVE** Cook the fettuccine in boiling salted water 4-6 minutes or until cooked to your preference. Add the cooked pasta to the skillet with the other ingredients. Season with salt and pepper and toss gently. Cook for 1 minute to allow the pasta to absorb flavor.

Serves 6

MARIO'S VIA ABRUZZI – THE COOKBOOK Our first foray into the realm of cookbook publishing came in 2001 when we released *Mario's Via Abruzzi – The Cookbook*, a volume consisting mainly of Abruzzese regional specialties with some Italian inspired creations of our own thrown in for good measure. After the book sold-out a few years later, rather than simply reprinting the old book, we developed an expanded 2nd edition. The expanded book was nearing completion when the project was shelved temporarily only to reemerge later as this book.

Fettuccine Mario

If there has been one dish that has been Mario Daniele's "go-to" recipe over the years whenever he is giving someone in the dining room the *extra*-special guest treatment it's this one. Usually he makes it himself but sometimes he'll call upon one of the Chefs to prepare it and everyone knows exactly what is meant by "we need an order of Fett Mario."

INGREDIENTS *One batch homemade fresh pasta (see page 76) or use 2-2½ lb store bought fresh fettuccine ‖ 1 quart heavy (whipping) cream ‖ 2 oz porcini mushrooms, dried ‖ 1 cup homemade chicken broth (see page 61) or used canned broth ‖ 1 lb mixed sliced mushrooms, chopped ‖ 2 shallots, chopped ‖ ½ cup extra-virgin olive oil ‖ ½ cup butter, unsalted ‖ ½ cup Italian flat leaf parsley, chopped ‖ To taste, crushed red pepper flakes ‖ To taste, Kosher salt and freshly ground pepper ‖ 1 cup parmigiano-reggiano or grana-padana cheese, grated ‖ 2 oz prepared ground truffle (optional)*

ONE Prepare one batch of homemade fresh pasta dough. Prepare the fettuccine using a hand-cranked pasta maker or Kitchen-Aid fettuccine attachment or use store bought pre-made fresh fettuccine. **TWO** Bring the cream to a boil over high heat in an oversized, heavy-bottomed saucepan. Cook the cream down to about half of its original volume. The cream will take on a distinct shine as it reduces to its proper thickness. Do not let the cream scorch on the bottom. Strain through a wire mesh strainer or cheesecloth to remove the porcini. Once the porcini have cooled enough to handle, chop them into small pieces and add them back to the cream. Season to taste with salt and white pepper. **THREE** Heat the olive oil in a large sauté pan over med-high heat. Add the chopped shallots and sauté for about 30 seconds, then add the butter and crushed red pepper. Sauté for about 1 minute to allow the shallots to soften. Add the mushrooms and sauté for 3-4 minutes until they are cooked. Season to taste with salt and pepper. Add the porcini cream reduction and chicken stock to the mushroom mixture. **FOUR** Cook the pasta in boiling salted water about 5-6 minutes or until cooked to your preference. Drain the pasta and add to the pan with the mushroom sauce. Season the pasta to taste with salt and pepper and toss the ingredients together. Add prepared ground truffle (optional). Toss and simmer briefly to allow the pasta to absorb the flavors. Add some of the pasta cooking water as needed to loosen if the dish becomes dry. Serve with freshly grated cheese.

Serves 6

A PASTA POINTER (NO. 1) We train all our Chefs to briefly simmer the pasta in the sauce before plating the dish. This technique is essential to making great pasta dishes at home because it gives the pasta a chance to absorb some of the flavor from the sauce. This is particularly important when making a pasta dish with a light sauce or a delicately flavored dish like this one.

Spaghetti *carbonara*

Our carbonara sauce is a simple variation on the classic. We use olive oil, pancetta, raw egg yolk, fresh cream, grated parmigiano-regianno and black pepper. Purists will point out that in Italy they would use cured pork jowl, or *guanciale* instead of pancetta and that carbonara does not traditionally have cream in it as shown below. The cream is a contemporary addition that we feel makes the raw egg more agreeable to the American palate. As for the *guanciale*, if you are able to track it down by all means use it; otherwise pancetta is a decent and much less costly substitute. Although the recipe is often embellished with other ingredients like peas or mushrooms to give the dish more substance we think it's best when kept simple.

INGREDIENTS *1½ lbs good quality spaghetti* ‖ *10-12 eggs* ‖ *1½ cup parmigiano-reggiano or grana-padana cheese* ‖ *2 tablespoons extra-virgin olive oil* ‖ *10 oz pancetta, sliced thin and chopped* ‖ *1 cup heavy (whipping) cream* ‖ *To taste, freshly ground pepper*

ONE Heat the oil over medium heat in a large sauté pan. Add the pancetta and cook for 6-7 minutes until some of the fat is rendered out and the pancetta begins to brown. Add the cream and reduce it by half over high heat. **TWO** In a large bowl, whisk together the egg and 1 cup of the cheese. **THREE** Cook the pasta in boiling salted water 8-10 minutes or until cooked to your preference. Drain and immediately toss together with the egg mixture, letting some of the pasta water carry into the pan with the pasta. Add the pancetta and cream mixture and freshly ground pepper to taste. Top with the additional cheese.

Serves 6

IS IT ABRUZZESE OR ROMAN (NO. 1)? This dish is thought to have originated during World War II in the hills outside of Rome by Italians who were being supplied bacon and eggs by the GI's. How exactly it came to be called *carbonara*, the Italian word for charcoal, is less clear. Some say it was created to feed Italian charcoal workers. Others suggest the flecks of bacon and black pepper in the dish resemble charcoal, while still others claim the dish was originally prepared by cooking it *over* charcoal. The debate also goes on in Italy as to whether the coal workers were in fact from Abruzzi, validating the claim that the dish is actually Abruzzese and not Roman.

Bucatini *Amatriciana*

Our favorite spaghetteria overlooks the magnificent *Piazza Duomo* in L'Aquila, Abruzzi. Our friend Carlo Capone, who owns the spaghetteria, taught us how to make this. A true Italian classic, we have featured this recipe not only on our menu but in just about every other way we possible could at one time or another including, our annual "pasta throw-down" where it crushed the competition in the voting. The traditional pasta of choice for this sauce is the long, tubular bucatini pasta. Carlo has also created his own version in which he adds the local saffron.

INGREDIENTS *1½ lb bucatini pasta ‖ 12 oz pancetta or guanciale ‖ 2 cups onion, chopped ‖ 1 teaspoon crushed red pepper ‖ 4 lb fresh plum (Roma) tomatoes or 2 (35 oz) can peeled tomatoes ‖ 1 cup dry white wine ‖ 1 cup extra-virgin olive oil ‖ To taste, Kosher salt and freshly ground pepper ‖ 1 cup freshly grated parmigiano-reggiano or pecorino-romano cheese*

ONE Use a paring knife to cut a small x in the top of the tomatoes. Submerge them in boiling water for about 1 minute or until the skins begin to blister. Remove and cool them down in ice water. Peel and cut in half. Gently squeeze out the seeds and chop. **TWO** Heat the olive oil over medium heat in a large skillet. Add the pancetta and cook for 6-8 minutes until the pancetta begins to brown. Add the onion and sauté for 5-6 more minutes to allow the onions to soften. Add the tomatoes, freshly ground pepper, and crushed red pepper. Sauté for 5 minutes before reducing the heat to low. Allow the sauce to simmer over low heat for 10 minutes. If you are using canned tomatoes, drain them, reserving the juice, and coarsely chop them before adding to the skillet. **TWO** Cook the pasta in boiling salted water about 8-10 minutes or until cooked to your preference. Drain the pasta, add it to the saucepan, and season to taste with salt and pepper. Toss and simmer briefly to allow the pasta to absorb the flavors. Use caution when adding the salt, given that the salt in the pancetta will contribute to the overall saltiness of the dish. If the dish becomes dry, add some of the pasta cooking water or reserved canned tomato juice as needed to moisten. Serve with freshly grated parmigiano-reggiano or pecorino-romano cheese.

Serves 6

IS IT ABRUZZESE OR ROMAN (NO. 2)? Amatrice is a small mountain village that borders the regions of Lazio and Abruzzi. The village is technically under the jurisdiction of Lazio, which means this celebrated sauce known the world over as *Amatriciana* is considered part of the cuisine of Lazio and Rome, its capital. This doesn't sit so well with some of the Chefs we know from Abruzzi who are quick to point out that Amatrice was part of the Abruzzi region until Mussolini redrew the map!

Pappardelle with sausage, peas & vodka sauce

To flame the alcohol or not to flame the alcohol? That is the question. Some Chefs advocate burning off the alcohol claiming that it's the enhancing effect of the alcohol, as it releases alcohol soluble flavors into the tomatoes and *not* the flavor of the vodka itself, that is important. Others say to you want to be able to taste the vodka and it should be added at the last minute so that the alcohol, which is what you are really tasting, doesn't get cooked out. Perhaps one should be called Vodka Sauce and the other Raw Vodka Sauce? A consistent favorite, this recipe has been featured on our menu for many years. If you make the vodka sauce from scratch you have the option to experiment with the vodka and decide for yourself, how you like it best.

INGREDIENTS *2½ lb wide fresh pasta ribbons pappardelle, or fresh fettuccine ‖ 1½ lb hot Italian sausage, bulk ‖ 1 lb peas, frozen ‖ 1 batch Mario's vodka sauce (see page 5) or use 3 jars of Mario's vodka sauce ‖ 1 cup ricotta cheese ‖ 6 oz butter, unsalted ‖ 1 tablespoon Italian parsley, chopped ‖ To taste, Kosher salt and freshly ground pepper ‖ ½ cup parmigiano-reggiano or grana-padana cheese, grated*

ONE Form the sausage into small marble-sized meatballs. Roast them on a sheet pan in a preheated 350° F oven for 5-7 minutes or until cooked throughout. **TWO** Heat a large skillet over medium heat. Add the sausage, the residual oil, and brown bits that are left on the sheet pan. Add the peas and vodka sauce and bring to a simmer. **THREE** Cook the pasta in boiling salted water about 5-6 minutes or until cooked to your preference. Drain the pasta and add it to the pan with vodka sauce. Season to taste with salt and freshly ground pepper. Add the butter and toss to combine. Simmer for 1 minute to allow the pasta to absorb the flavors. If the dish becomes dry, add some of the pasta cooking water as needed to loosen. Serve promptly, topped with a dollop of ricotta and freshly grated cheese.

Serves 6

MARIO'S VODKA SAUCE The idea of spiking tomato sauce with vodka and smoothing it out with added cream is a relatively recent one, dating from the early 1980s when it was considered part of the New Cuisine or *nuevo cucina* trend that was fashionable in Italy at that time. It quickly found its way to America where it has remained an enduring favorite and a best seller at grocery stores. We added Mario's Vodka Sauce to our sauce line-up in 2006.

Rigatoni *Bolognese*

To many Americans *Bolognese* sauce is basically ground beef simmered in red sauce. To be sure, one can brown-off ground beef with onions, garlic and herbs, add some kind of tomato product and a splash of wine to come up with a decent tasting sauce but this is a far cry from a traditional meat sauce in the style of Bologna, or *Ragu alla Bolognese*. This recipe is the real deal.

INGREDIENTS *1½ lb rigatoni pasta ‖ 1½ lb ground beef ‖ ½ lb ground pork ‖ ½ lb ground veal ‖ 4 oz chicken livers ‖ 2 bay leaves ‖ 1 cup onion, rough chopped ‖ 1 cup celery, rough chopped ‖ 1 cup carrot, rough chopped ‖ 6 cloves garlic ‖ 2 tablespoons Italian parsley, chopped ‖ ¾ cup extra-virgin olive oil ‖ 2-3 pinches dry oregano ‖ 3 cups dry red wine ‖ 2 (28 oz) cans crushed tomatoes ‖ 2 cups heavy cream ‖ 4 tablespoons butter, unsalted ‖ 1 cup parmigiano or grana-padana cheese, grated ‖ To taste, Kosher salt and freshly ground black pepper*

ONE Put the onion, celery, carrot, and garlic into a food processor and pulse until finely and evenly chopped. Remove and set aside. Put the chicken livers into the food processor and pulse until smooth. Remove and set aside. **TWO** Heat a large skillet over high heat. Add the meats to the skillet and cook over high heat to brown, breaking them down as you go. Season the meat to taste with salt and pepper. Transfer to a colander to drain and cool. **THREE** Heat the olive oil and bay leaf over medium heat. Add the ground vegetables and cook for 5 minutes or until they begin to soften. Push the vegetables to the side of the pan and add the chicken livers to the empty side. Cook for 5 more minutes or until cooked throughout. Return the browned meats to the skillet and add the oregano and red wine. Simmer 5 minutes. Add the crushed tomato and simmer an additional 20 minutes to allow the flavors to develop. Add the cream and butter and season to taste with salt and pepper. **FOUR** Cook the pasta in boiling salted water about 8-10 minutes or until done to your preference. Drain the pasta and add to the pan with the sauce. Season the pasta to taste with salt and pepper. Toss and simmer briefly to allow the pasta to absorb the flavors. If the dish becomes dry, add some of the pasta cooking water as needed to loosen. Serve with freshly grated parmigiano or grana-padana cheese.

Serves 6

DON'T SKIP THE CHICKEN LIVERS! You'll notice that we use chicken livers here. The use of chicken livers was controversial when we first started running this recipe in 1996, so we took a poll and blind tested over fifty staff members and customers by having them sample the sauce with and sans chicken livers. We never mentioned that there were livers in the sauce and only asked that they identify which sauce they preferred. Overwhelmingly, something like 55 votes-to-4, the preferred sauce was the one with chicken livers in it. If you are strongly averse to chicken livers don't use them, but trust us they only serve to give enhance and deepen the flavor profile; if we didn't tell you, you wouldn't know they were in there.

Spaghetti with *ragú di bianco*

Here we have a *ragú di bianco*, or "white meat sauce" named so because only white meats, chicken, veal and pork, and no tomato products are used in the preparation. This dish has been on the menu a couple of different times and we consistently get special requests to make it.

INGREDIENTS *1½ lb spaghetti pasta* ‖ *¾ lb ground chicken* ‖ *¾ lb ground veal* ‖ *¾ lb ground pork* ‖ *6 oz pancetta, sliced thin and chopped fine* ‖ *1½ cup carrot, peeled and roughly chopped* ‖ *1½ cup onion, peeled and roughly chopped* ‖ *1½ cup celery, peeled and roughly chopped* ‖ *2 cups extra-virgin olive oil* ‖ *1 cup chicken broth (see page 61) or canned broth* ‖ *1 cup dry white wine* ‖ *3 hot pepper pods* ‖ *1 teaspoon garlic, finely chopped* ‖ *To taste, Kosher salt and freshly ground pepper* ‖ *1 cup parmigiano-reggiano or grana-padana cheese, grated* ‖ *4-5 oz Italian prepared ground truffle, or to taste (optional)*

ONE Put the onion, celery, carrot, and garlic into a food processor and pulse until finely and evenly chopped. Remove and set aside. **TWO** Heat the olive oil over medium heat in a large skillet. Add the pancetta and cook for 6-8 minutes until the pancetta begins to brown. Remove the pancetta using a slotted spoon or strainer. Add the meats and hot pepper pods to the skillet and cook over high heat, breaking them up as they cook. As the meat cooks it will release water. This water will evaporate quickly and afterwards the meats will begin to properly brown. This will take 15-20 total minutes. **THREE** Once the meats have browned, remove them from the skillet using a slotted spoon or strainer, leaving behind the oil and any pan drippings. Add the carrot, onion, celery, and garlic to the skillet and cook over medium heat for 8-10 minutes or until the vegetables soften. **FOUR** Add the meats and pancetta back to the pan along with the wine and chicken stock. Simmer for 10 additional minutes to allow the flavor to develop. Season to taste with salt and pepper. **FIVE** Cook the pasta in boiling salted water about 8-10 minutes or until cooked to your preference. Drain the pasta and add to the pan with the sauce. Season the pasta to taste with salt and pepper. Toss and simmer briefly to allow the pasta to absorb the flavors. If the dish becomes dry, add some of the pasta cooking water as needed to loosen. Serve with freshly grated parmigiano-reggiano or grana-padana cheese. If possible, seek out ground truffles to toss in at the end with the pasta and sauce.

Serves 6

THANKS DOMINGO! We learned how to make this dish on our second staff trip to Italy at Garden of the Princes, or *Giardinera di Principi*, a lovely hotel and restaurant in Abruzzi, Italy. Owner and Chef, Domingo Fiorino, graciously spent a full day teaching (and feeding) us his wonderful cuisine. The spaghetti cartoccio in this book is another recipe we learned from Domingo.

Spaghetti *cartoccio*

This recipe, a seafood pasta dish presented in a foil sleeve, is one of our signature dishes having remained on the menu since 2001. The foil sleeve, or *cartoccio*, allows you to put it aside in the oven for a few minutes so that you can attend to your guests before presentation. When you cut open the foil the steamy aroma of garlic, tomatoes and seafood are sure to earn you a few "Wows!"

INGREDIENTS *1½ lb spaghetti pasta* ‖ *2 dozen littleneck clams* ‖ *1 lb black mussels* ‖ *1½ cup clam juice* ‖ *1½ cup extra-virgin olive oil* ‖ *1 tablespoon chopped garlic* ‖ *6 hot pepper pods* ‖ *3 tablespoons Italian parsley, chopped* ‖ *1 can (28 oz) crushed tomatoes* ‖ *1 can (18 oz) chopped tomatoes* ‖ *2 tablespoons Italian parsley, chopped* ‖ *2 anchovy filets, smashed* ‖ *18 jumbo shrimp, peeled & de-veined* ‖ *18 scallops* ‖ *1 lb squid, cut into rings with tentacles, cleaned* ‖ *To taste, Kosher salt and freshly ground pepper* ‖ *18-inch wide foil*

ONE Wash and pick through the clams and mussels, discarding any that will not close when tapped gently or that have an off odor. Set aside the mussels and put the clams in a large pot with the clam juice. Cover and simmer over medium heat until all the clams open. Discard any that do not open. **TWO** Heat the olive oil in a large heavy-bottomed skillet over medium-high heat. Add the garlic and hot peppers. Continue to fry the garlic until it becomes golden brown in color. Add half the parsley, It should sizzle when added to the oil. Quickly add the crushed and diced tomatoes along with the anchovy paste and simmer over low heat for 10 minutes. Add the shrimp, scallops, mussels, and squid to the pot along with the opened clams and all the juice from the clam pot. Simmer until all the seafood is *just* cooked. **THREE** Cook the pasta in boiling salted water about 8-10 minutes or until cooked to your preference. Drain the pasta and add to the pan with the seafood. Season the pasta to taste with salt and pepper. Toss and simmer briefly to allow the pasta to absorb the flavors. If the dish becomes dry, add some of the pasta cooking water as needed to loosen. **FOUR** For the cartoccio: Take two 4-foot lengths of 18-inch wide foil. Fold each piece in half lengthwise and center them on two large plates or platters. Open up the folded foil and place half of the pasta in the center of each. Pour the seafood over the pasta, dividing the ingredients evenly. Garnish with freshly chopped parsley. Crimp around the edges completely, sealing the foil except for a small opening. Insert a blow dryer into the opening and blow up the sleeve.

Serves 6

DON'T SKIP THE MUSSELS AND SQUID! Authentic ingredients go a long way toward achieving that illusive authentic flavor you experienced while traveling abroad or dining at a good Italian restaurant. In the case of seafood dishes like this one authenticity is only a few mussels and a handful of squid away. That's right, these two humble, often maligned ingredients, are as ubiquitous as parsley in Italian seafood dishes. As they simmer together with other more glamorous seafood and fish, like shrimp and scallops, they transform the dish into the one you'll swear tastes exactly like that dish you had in Italy.

Spaghetti *Posillipo*

It's fair to say that old-school Italian-American dishes like this have to some extent gone out of style, but the fact remains people will always love pasta with seafood and a healthy dose of garlic. For some people a dish like this is the *only thing* that will satisfy a craving for Italian food. Use whatever seafood you like and feel free to go heavy on the garlic. Garlic is one of those few things in life that is as good as it is good for you! Oregano adds a decidedly Southern Italian element to this dish, as does the tomato and garlic which is why similarly flavored dishes are often called *Posillipo*, the name of a point of land on the Bay of Naples.

INGREDIENTS *1½ lb spaghetti* ‖ *18 littleneck clams* ‖ *1 lb black mussels* ‖ *1½ cup clam juice* ‖ *1 pound sea scallops* ‖ *1 pound raw jumbo shrimp, peeled and de-veined* ‖ *2 cups olive oil* ‖ *6 cloves garlic, peeled and chopped* ‖ *1½ lb plum tomatoes* ‖ *½ cup Italian parsley, chopped* ‖ *2-3 pinches dried oregano (optional)* ‖ *4-6 dried hot pepper pods, or crushed red pepper* ‖ *To taste, sea salt and freshly ground pepper*

ONE Using a paring knife, cut a small x in the top of the tomatoes. Submerge them in boiling water for about 1 minute or until the skins begin to blister. Remove and cool them in ice water. Peel and cut in half. Gently squeeze out the seeds and chop. **TWO** Wash and pick through the clams and mussels, discarding any that will not close when tapped gently or that have an off odor. Set aside the mussels and put the clams in a large pot with the clam juice. Cover and simmer over medium heat until all the clams open. Discard any that do not open or have an off odor. **THREE** Heat the olive oil over medium-high heat in a large skillet. Add the garlic and fry briefly, allowing it to take on a slightly toasted color. Add the parsley and hot pepper pods. The parsley should sizzle when added to the pan. Add the remaining seafood, tomatoes, and oregano. Sauté for 5 minutes before reducing the heat to low. Add the clams and the clam cooking water to the pan. Season the to taste with salt and pepper. **FOUR** Cook the pasta in boiling salted water about 8-10 minutes or until cooked to your preference. Drain the pasta and add it to the pan with the seafood. Season to taste with salt and pepper. Toss and simmer briefly to allow the pasta to absorb the flavors. If the dish becomes dry, add some of the pasta cooking water as needed to loosen.

Serves 6

A BYGONE ERA This dish evokes the bygone era when red checkered tablecloths and Chianti bottles accentuated the dining rooms of American-Italian restaurants like *Mario's Pizza & Pasta* on East Avenue. Back then, most Americans perceived Italian food as just another inexpensive ethnic food on the same order as take-out Chinese food: beloved by many, but not always respected. Then in the 1980's there was a craze for Northern Italian food: Italian cuisine was suddenly taken seriously and ingredients like risotto and polenta, despite having very humble origins, were appearing on the menus of the most upscale and sophisticated restaurants in America. It was this culinary movement and the newfound appreciation for *la vera cucina*, the real cuisine, of Italy that really set the stage for the Daniele family to open *Mario's Via Abruzzi* in 1995.

Linguine with shrimp, tomatoes, fennel and lentils

Lentils, or *lenticche*, are grown in many regions of Italy. Among the most highly prized are the ones harvested in Abruzzi, where pulses and legumes are an important part of the cuisine. This pasta dish features brown lentils with fresh fennel and shrimp. It may sound like an unusual combination but trust us, this dish never disappoints.

INGREDIENTS *1½ lb linguine pasta* ‖ *1 lb brown (French) lentils, or substitute regular lentils* ‖ *1¼ cup extra virgin olive oil* ‖ *¼ lb pancetta, thinly sliced and chopped* ‖ *3 bay leaves* ‖ *6 cloves garlic* ‖ *1 cup onion, chopped* ‖ *2 quarts homemade chicken broth (see page 61) or use canned broth* ‖ *1 batch Abruzzese tomato sauce (see page 5)* ‖ *2 bulbs fresh fennel* ‖ *2 lb large shrimp, peeled and de-veined* ‖ *To taste, sea salt and freshly ground pepper*

ONE Pick through the lentils to remove stones or other debris and wash them. Heat ½ cup of the olive oil over medium heat in a large saucepan. Add the pancetta and cook for 6-8 minutes until the pancetta begins to brown. Add the bay leaf and garlic cloves and fry for about one minute or until the garlic is cooked. Add the onion and sauté for 2-3 minutes. Add the lentils to the pan together with the water or chicken stock. Cook the lentils for 45 minutes or until tender. Season to taste with salt and pepper. Strain the lentils, reserving the liquid, and remove the bay leaves and whole garlic cloves. Spread them out on a sheet pan to cool. **TWO** Cut the fennel down the middle and remove the core before thinly slicing lengthwise. Blanch the fennel in boiling water for 1 minute. Remove and set aside. **THREE** Heat up the remaining oil in a large skillet over medium heat. Sauté the shrimp 3-4 minutes or until they are *just* done. Add the cooked lentils, blanched fennel and Abruzzi sauce to the pan and toss gently to heat throughout. **FOUR** Cook the pasta in boiling salted water about 8-10 minutes or until cooked to your preference. Drain the pasta and add to the pan with the shrimp. Season the pasta to taste with salt and pepper. Toss and simmer briefly to allow the pasta to absorb the flavors. If the dish becomes too dry at this point add some of the reserved liquid from the lentils to loosen.

Serves 6

A PASTA POINTER (NO. 2) Here is our advice for cooking pasta. First, always cook pasta in plenty of water. It has to have room to expand and the released starch needs to wash away. Secondly, make sure the water is at a rolling boil before adding the pasta. When it comes to a boil again then turn it down to a simmer. It will turn out pasty otherwise. Lastly, always salt the water. A good rule of thumb is 1 tablespoon for every 3 quarts of water. Don't expect the sauce to season the pasta.

Linguine with clams and mussels

This dish calls for a mixture of Littlenecks, New Zealand cockle clams and black mussels. If you can find New Zealand cockles, which are small and tender, much like the clams they would use in Italy, by all means use them, if not frozen whole baby clams will do or just use more littlenecks. We watched this dish being prepared many times when were in Italy because it's one of our favorites and we wanted to get it right.

INGREDIENTS *1½ lb linguine pasta ‖ 2 dozen littleneck clams ‖ 1 lb New Zealand cockle clams or frozen whole baby clams ‖ 1 lb Prince Edward Island black mussels ‖ 2½ cups extra-virgin olive oil ‖ 3 tablespoons fresh chopped garlic ‖ 3 tablespoons fresh chopped parsley ‖ 3 pinches crushed red pepper ‖ 6 cups clam juice ‖ To taste, Kosher salt and freshly ground pepper*

ONE Wash and pick through the clams and mussels, discarding any that will not close when tapped gently or that have an off odor. **TWO** Heat the olive oil in a large skillet, add the garlic and fry it in the oil for about 30 seconds or until it begins to toast lightly. Quickly add about half of the parsley and the crushed red pepper flakes. Add the clam juice. Place the clams into the pan and cover, simmering for 2 minutes before adding the mussels. Simmer until all the shells open. Discard any shells that do not open or have an off odor. **THREE** Cook the pasta in boiling salted water about 8-10 minutes or until cooked to your preference. Drain the pasta and add to the pan with the clams. Season the pasta to taste with salt and pepper. Toss and simmer briefly to allow the pasta to absorb the flavors. If the dish becomes dry, add some of the pasta cooking water as needed to loosen.

Serves 6

A PASTA POINTER (NO. 3) When making pasta dishes like this one you want to have the proper ratio of oil to liquid in order to keep the sauce from being either oily or watery. You know you've gotten it right when the oil and liquid become suspended and little droplets of oil are formed on the surface. In Italy they call these eyes, or *occhi*. In general that means a 1:2 ratio of oil to liquid, but sometimes the liquid evaporates or is absorbed by the pasta so it's always best to look for the eyes if you want to get it right.

Maltagliati (badly cut pasta) with shrimp and scallops

This dish became an instant hit with our staff when we were shown how to make it on our first staff trip to Italy. We quickly to put it on *Mario's* menu when we returned and it became an instant success with our customers as well. The unexpected addition of arugula is what sets this dish apart. Use the more flavorful baby arugula if you can find it, and don't be shy with it either. If you love seafood and arugula then you are going to love this recipe.

INGREDIENTS *1 batch homemade fresh pasta (see page 76) or use 2-2½ lb pre-made fresh fettuccine* ‖ *1 pound large shrimp, peeled and de-veined* ‖ *1 pound sea scallops* ‖ *3 cups extra-virgin olive oil* ‖ *4½ cups clam juice* ‖ *4 cups plum tomatoes, diced* ‖ *3 tablespoons shallots, chopped* ‖ *1 banana or Italian hot green pepper, seeds removed and sliced (optional)* ‖ *2 cups arugula, coarsely chopped* ‖ *To taste, Kosher salt and freshly ground pepper* ‖ *Additional fresh arugula, for garnish*

ONE Prepare one batch of homemade fresh pasta sheets using a hand-cranked pasta maker or Kitchen-Aid attachment adjusted to a medium setting. Cut the pasta into random pieces and strips. **TWO** Heat the olive oil in a large skillet, over medium heat. Add the chopped shallot, sliced hot pepper and 1 cup of the chopped arugula and sauté for 2 minutes. Add the shrimp, scallops, and tomatoes and cook for 2 more minutes, allowing the flavors to develop. Add the clam juice and continue to cook until the seafood and tomatoes are *just* cooked. Season with salt and pepper and add the remaining chopped arugula. **THREE** Cook the pasta in boiling salted water about 8-10 minutes or until cooked to your preference. Drain the pasta and add to the pan with the seafood. Season the pasta to taste with salt and pepper. Toss and simmer briefly to allow the pasta to absorb the flavors. If the dish becomes dry, add some of the pasta cooking water as needed to loosen. Top with additional arugula leaves and serve.

Serves 6

BADLY CUT PASTA Badly cut pasta, or *maltagliati* in Italian, refers to the random strips and trimmed bits of pasta that are the byproduct of making lasagne, ravioli, and other fresh pastas. The malformed cuts have become trendy in the Abruzzi region of Italy where the "shape" is popular enough to be considered a regional specialty. We could never generate enough lasagne and ravioli byproduct to meet the demand for this dish, so we use another trick we learned in Italy: we rolled up our homemade sheets and cut them badly on purpose.

Seafood risotto

Chef James Dean makes this classic seafood risotto dish for some of our regulars who insist that he, and only he can make the way they like it. James advises us, "making good risotto is a labor of love that requires constant stirring and attention." He also stresses the fact that "to cook properly the liquid should be added slowly, as it is absorbed." This is how James makes it.

INGREDIENTS *2 cups Arborio rice ‖ 1 cup clam juice ‖ 1 cup tomato juice ‖ 1 cup Mario's pasta sauce ‖ ½ cup dry white wine ‖ 2 plum tomatoes, chopped ‖ ½ cup onions, chopped ‖ ½ cup red bell peppers, diced ‖ ½ cup green peppers, diced ‖ ½ cup celery, diced ‖ 4 ounces whole butter ‖ 3 cloves garlic, chopped ‖ 3-4 anchovies, smashed ‖ ½ cup parsley, chopped ‖ ½ cup basil, chopped ‖ 2 bay leaves ‖ 4-5 hot dry chili peppers or crushed red chilis to taste ‖ ¼ teaspoon Thai fish sauce ‖ ¼ cup extra-virgin olive oil ‖ ½ lb jumbo shrimp, peeled and de-veined ‖ 8 oz scallops ‖ 12 black mussels ‖ 12 littleneck clams ‖ 1 lb squid, cut into rings and tentacles, and cleaned ‖ To taste, sea salt and freshly ground pepper*

ONE Melt 2 ounces of butter over medium heat in a large heavy-bottomed saucepan. Add the bay leaf, hot peppers, onion, and anchovy. Sauté until the onions are soft. Turn the heat up to medium-high and add the rice. Stir the rice constantly, preferably using a wooden spoon to avoid breaking up the rice, for about 3-4 minutes. Add the peppers, celery, and garlic and continue to cook until they soften. Add the white wine. Let the rice absorb the wine. **TWO** Mix to combine the clam juice, tomato juice, and Mario's pasta sauce into a suitably sized container. Reduce the heat to low and add this mixture to the rice, about ½ cup at a time, allowing the liquid to become absorbed before adding additional liquid. **THREE** In a separate sauté pan, heat the olive oil over high heat. Add the shrimp, scallops, and clams, and sauté these about half way before adding the mussels. Once the shellfish has opened, turn the heat down to medium and simmer an additional 1-2 minutes to cook. **FOUR** Meanwhile, continue adding stock to the rice as needed. Once the rice has cooked al dente, add the contents of the shellfish pan, the squid, and about half of the basil and parsley. Continue an additional 3-4 minutes or until the squid is cooked throughout. **FIVE** Season to taste with salt and pepper and stir in the remaining butter and olive oil. Garnish with the remaining basil and parsley.

Serves 6

ITALIAN RICE Try to purchase risotto from the grocery store and the first thing you'll notice is the fact that you can't find risotto. This is because risotto is not a type of rice but rather a *rice dish* made with Italian short grain rice. Arborio is the most commonly available Italian rice but others such as Carnarolli and Vialone Nano are becoming increasingly available. When purchasing Italian rice, for best results buy good quality, preferably imported product and avoid generic domestic rice that tend to become gluey.

Specialta di Montanara— meat and poultry

Anthony Daniele with Nonnetta Esilde (Mario's Mother) 2009

Chicken porcini

This chicken recipe is one of a quartet of chicken dishes that have all been very popular signature menu items for us at one time, or another. (The other three chicken recipes are also in this book) This one is a twist on the classic combination of sautéed chicken breast and porcini mushrooms only it's done our way with added brandy and cream. The end result is chicken enrobed in creamy, garlicky, mushroomy goodness.

INGREDIENTS *3-4 lb chicken breast, rinsed* ‖ *2 cups all-purpose flour* ‖ *1 lb mixed portobello, domestic and shiitake mushrooms, sliced* ‖ *1 cup salad oil* ‖ *1 cup brandy* ‖ *2½ cups porcini cream sauce* ‖ *3 tablespoons unsalted butter* ‖ *To taste, Kosher salt and freshly ground black pepper*

PORCINI CREAM SAUCE *4 cups heavy (whipping) cream* ‖ *1 oz dry porcini mushrooms* ‖ *1 cup veal demi-glace (available at most good grocery stores)* ‖ *¼ cup olive oil* ‖ *2 tablespoons garlic, chopped* ‖ *2 tablespoons shallots, chopped* ‖ *1 tablespoon Italian parsley, chopped*

ONE Trim the fat from the chicken breast. Cut and pound it out evenly using a meat mallet as needed to facilitate sautéing. **TWO** For the porcini cream sauce: Pre-soak the dried porcini in a minimal amount of warm water for one hour. Remove the hydrated porcini and chop fine. Reserve the porcini water. Heat the olive oil in large saucepan, add the garlic and fry briefly to obtain a golden brown color. Add the chopped parsley and shallots and sauté to soften the shallots. Add the heavy cream and the chopped porcini, together with the reserved porcini water. Bring the mixture to a boil and simmer over high heat until it cooks down and begins to thicken. **THREE** Heat the salad oil in a large sauté pan over moderate heat. Season the chicken with salt and pepper and dredge in lightly seasoned flour. Shake off the excess flour. Carefully place the chicken in the pan and sauté to obtain a nice golden brown-color on one side. **FOUR** Turn over the chicken and add the mushroom mix to the pan. Continue to sauté to until the chicken is cooked throughout and the mushrooms soften. Drain the excess oil from the pan. **FIVE** Turn the heat up to high for 30 seconds before adding the brandy. Allow the alcohol to cook off before adding the porcini cream sauce a pinch of parsley. Warm throughout and season to taste with salt and pepper. Swirl in the butter to finish.

Serves 6

COOKING WITH DRY PORCINI While tough and practically inedible when dry, porcini re-hydrate fairly well after an hour or so in warm water. In so doing, the hydrating liquid becomes infused with a deep porcini mushroom flavor. This liquid should always be incorporated into any recipe calling for dry porcini.

Pollo Aquilano This chicken recipe was inspired by a similar dish they serve at *Ristorante La Tre Marie*, in L'Aquila, the picturesque medieval city that is the capital of Abruzzi. At *La Tre Marie* they serve a lightly battered chicken breast that is layered with ham and melted cheese, and finished with a rich chicken based sauce. We decided to substitute prosciutto for the ham and this became the signature chicken dish on our menu for several years.

INGREDIENTS *3-4 lb chicken breast, rinsed ‖ 2-2 ½ cups all-purpose flour ‖ 6 large eggs ‖ 3 tablespoons water ‖ ⅓ cup vegetable oil ‖ 4 slices prosciutto ‖ 4 slices mozzarella cheese ‖ ½ cup dry white wine ‖ 12 fresh sage leaves ‖ 2 tablespoons unsalted butter ‖ To taste, Kosher salt and ground pepper*

CHICKEN SAUCE (BASIC VELOUTE) *3 cups homemade chicken broth (see page 61) or use canned broth ‖ ½ cup diced carrot ‖ ½ cup diced onion ‖ ½ cup diced celery ‖ 2 tablespoons vegetable oil ‖ 2 tablespoon all-purpose flour ‖ ⅓ cup clarified butter ‖ To taste, Kosher salt and ground pepper*

ONE Trim the fat from the chicken breast. Cut and pound it out evenly using a meat mallet as needed to facilitate sautéing. **TWO** To make the chicken sauce: Heat the oil in a saucepan over moderate heat. Add the carrot, onion, and celery. Sauté for several minutes, until the vegetables soften and brown slightly. Add the clarified butter and flour. Mix to form a paste or roux. Cook for about 5 minutes over low heat. Whisk in the chicken stock and simmer for 20 minutes. Strain and season to taste with salt and pepper. **THREE** Make a batter by whisking the eggs with ½ cup of flour. Whisk the water into the mixture. The mix should form a thin batter. Season with salt and pepper to taste. **FOUR** Heat the oil in a large sauté pan over moderate heat. Season the chicken breasts with salt and pepper before coating them with flour. Shake off the excess flour and dip them into the batter. Quickly transfer the chicken to the pan and sauté for 3 minutes to set the batter and obtain and nice color. Turn the chicken over and sauté over low heat for 5-6 more minutes or until cooked throughout. **FOUR** Drain the oil from the pan and add the white wine and fresh sage leaves. Layer each chicken breast with sliced prosciutto and mozzarella and cover the pan. Warm over low heat to melt the cheese. Remove the chicken to a serving plate. Add the sauce to the pan and bring to a simmer. Swirl the butter into the pan with the sauce and pour over the chicken.

Serves 6

BATTER UP! The lightness of the batter is what we initially found to be intriguing when we tried a version of this dish in Italy. Chicken breasts are usually floured, breaded, or egg-dipped before they are sautéed.

Chicken *balsamico*

In this recipe, sautéed chicken breast and julienne vegetables are briefly simmered in our signature balsamic demi-glace. Our balsamic demi-glace is a simple preparation consisting of balsamic vinegar and veal demi-glace cooked down with herbs and added Dijon mustard. It is probably deserving of its own recipe page since we have used it so often and in so many dishes. Try it with added raisins and toasted pine nuts, over sliced roasted pork or all by itself as a simple steak sauce with any cut of beef, veal or lamb.

INGREDIENTS *3-4 lb chicken breast, rinsed* ‖ *2 cups all-purpose flour* ‖ *1 cup salad oil* ‖ *2 cups balsamic demi-glace* ‖ *1 cup heavy (whipping cream)* ‖ *2 large zucchini* ‖ *2 large yellow squash* ‖ *2 carrots* ‖ *3 tablespoons unsalted butter* ‖ *To taste, Kosher salt and freshly ground pepper*

BALSAMIC DEMI-GLACE *3 cups balsamic vinegar* ‖ *1 cup veal demi-glace (available at good grocery stores)* ‖ *1 small bay leaf* ‖ *1 sprig fresh rosemary, about 1 inch* ‖ *1 tablespoon Dijon mustard* ‖ *To taste, Kosher salt and freshly ground pepper*

ONE Trim the fat off the chicken breast. Cut and pound it out evenly using a meat mallet as needed to facilitate sautéing. **TWO** For the balsamic demi-glace: Bring the vinegar to a boil over high heat in a large heavy-bottomed pot. When the vinegar boils down by about half, add the veal demi-glace, bay leaf, and rosemary. Continue to boil until the glace is thick enough to coat the back of a spoon. Whisk the Dijon mustard into the sauce and season to taste with salt and pepper. Strain through a wire mesh strainer or cheesecloth. **THREE** Wash the squash and, using a mandoline, cut into fine julienne strands, 3-4 inches in length. Peel the carrots and cut them the same as the squash. Blanch the carrots in boiling water for 30 seconds before adding them to the squash. **FOUR** Heat about half of the oil in a large sauté pan over moderate heat. Season the chicken breasts with salt and pepper and dredge them in flour. Shake off the excess flour and carefully place the chicken in the pan. Sauté to obtain a nice golden brown color on one side. Turn over and continue cooking until the chicken is cooked throughout. Transfer to a plate for holding. **FIVE** Wipe the pan and warm the remaining oil over moderate heat. Add the zucchini, yellow squash, and carrots to the pan and sauté to soften. Drain off the oil and season to taste with salt and pepper. Return the chicken to the pan and add the balsamic demi-glace. Warm throughout and toss with the butter before serving.

Serves 6

PRE-MADE BALSAMIC GLAZE There are several balsamic glazes on the market. Usually these are cooked down mixtures of vinegar and corn syrup with added flavors. These glazes pair well with fruits, like cantaloupe and strawberries and they are excellent drizzled onto mixed grilled vegetables. However, they are typically too sharp for a dish like this one where the tartness of the vinegar tends to be overpowering.

Chicken under a brick, devil style

Cooking chicken under a flat stone is an ancient Italian cooking method that dates back to Etruscan Italy, an era that ended roughly around 500 BC. This method may seem a bit exotic but it's simply a matter of having bricks and a frying pan to prepare chicken this way. We add a good amount of crushed red pepper to the marinade which makes it devil or *diavolo* style.

INGREDIENTS *2 whole chickens ‖ ½ cup extra-virgin olive oil ‖ 3 tablespoons fresh garlic, chopped ‖ 1 tablespoon crushed red pepper flakes ‖ 2 lemons, juiced ‖ 1 tablespoon fresh thyme, picked from the stem ‖ 1 tablespoon fresh rosemary, stripped from the stem and chopped ‖ To taste, sea salt ‖ 1 lemon cut into wedges*

ONE To prepare the chicken: Lay the bird on its back and locate the breastbone in the center with your hand, noting the two breasts on either side. Take a good sharp utility or boning knife and cut down the length of one side of the breastbone. Use small slashing strokes and try to get as close to the bone as possible. Near the top of the breast, the end closest to the neck, you will encounter the wishbone, cut right through this. At this point you should have a slit going down the length of the breast close to the bone. Continue to cut away the breast meat, taking care to cut in smooth strokes close to or against the rib cage as you work your way down. Cut away the breast and the thigh taking care to keep the two pieces intact. Cut through the joint where the leg meets the backbone. Cut out and remove the thighbone. You should now have a semi-boneless half-chicken, the only remaining bones should be the lower part of the leg and the wings. Prepare the remaining chicken this way. **TWO** Combine the oil, garlic, crushed red pepper, lemon juice, thyme, rosemary, and salt and pepper to taste in a shallow non-reactive dish and add the chicken. Cover and marinate overnight or for at least 2 hours. **THREE** Double wrap two standard sized bricks in aluminum foil, shiny side out. **FOUR** Remove the chicken from the marinade. Heat a large cast iron or Teflon skillet over medium-high heat. Add a thin layer of salad oil to the skillet. Place two chicken halves skin side down in the pan and quickly place the bricks on top. Cook for 12-15 minutes or until the skin is very crispy. Repeat with the other two half-chickens and set all four halves on a sheet pan. **FIVE** Roast in a 400° F oven for an additional 10-15 minutes or until the chicken is cooked throughout. The exact cooking time will vary depending on the size of the bird. For optimal moistness, remove the chicken from the oven when it is *just* done. Serve with fresh lemon wedges.

Serves 6

GIMMIE SOME SKIN! (NO. 1) What makes this technique special is the way the skin flattens out and crisps up when pressure from the brick is applied. The secret here is to place the chicken skin-side down in the pan and then immediately place a foil wrapped brick, or other similarly heavy weight, on the chicken before the skin has had a chance to contract.

Honey roasted duck with sun-dried cherry & grappa sauce

This duck recipe does not exactly fall into the meals-in-minutes category but it's actually very easy to pull off. A dish that's sure to impress, it's also perfect for entertaining since the duck and sauce can be prepared ahead of time. We featured this duck recipe on our menu for a couple of years in the late 1990's and it was so well received that it inspired a spin-off recipe with sautéed veal.

INGREDIENTS *3 whole duck ‖ 3 oranges ‖ 3 medium onions ‖ 3 fresh rosemary sprigs ‖ 2 cups honey ‖ 1 cup soy sauce ‖ To taste, Kosher salt and freshly ground black pepper ‖ 3 cups duck, veal, or chicken demi-glace ‖ 4 oz sun-dried cherries ‖ 1½ cup triple-sec ‖ ½ cup grappa ‖ 4 oz unsalted butter ‖ ½ cup soy sauce ‖ 2 cups salad oil*

ONE Rinse out the ducks out with water. Reserve the neck bones. Using a knife, remove the "V" shaped tip of the wing. Drizzle the honey equally inside each bird and season the cavities with salt and pepper. Cut the oranges and onions in half and insert them into the ducks with a rosemary sprig. **TWO** Place the ducks, neck bones, and wing tips into a roasting pan or broiling dish, preferably fitted with a wire rack. Rub soy sauce around the outside of each duck. Roast at 250° F for 1 hour and 45 minutes or until the juices run clear when the thigh is pierced. Set aside to cool. **THREE** For the sauce: Once the ducks have cooled enough to handle, cut them in half by first cutting down the backside along the spine and then drawing a knife between the two breasts to separate the halves. Reserve the orange, onion and rosemary. Remove the backbone. Using your hands, carefully remove the rib cage, thigh, and other bones so you are left with only the leg and wing bones intact. Place all the bones, roasted necks, wing tips, reserved onions, oranges, and rosemary springs, into a large pot. Add the demi-glace and a minimal amount of water to cover. Simmer for 90 minutes before straining through a fine wire mesh strainer or cheesecloth into thick-bottomed saucepot. Bring the contents to a boil and cook down to obtain a sauce consistency. Add triple-sec and cook down again before adding the grappa and sun dried-cherries. Stir in the butter to finish and remove from the heat. **FOUR** Place the ducks on a roasting pan and into a 350° F degree oven to heat throughout. Heat the salad oil in a sauté pan over high heat. The oil should be between ¼ and ½ inch deep. Once the oil becomes very hot, but not in danger of smoking, take each duck half and place it skin side down in the oil, allowing the skin to fry and crisp up for about 30 seconds. Serve with the sauce.

Serves 6

FAQ (NO. 2) What is grappa? Grappa is a distilled spirit made from the residual grape seeds and skins that are a byproduct of wine making. Commonly served in Italian restaurants as an after dinner drink, or *digestivo*, grappa can be purchased at most liquor stores.

Roasted rabbit with porcini mushroom and black truffle sauce

Porcini and truffle may seem like overrated and expensive ingredients to the uninitiated, but to the enlightened they are the crown jewels of Italian cuisine. The ultimate would be to use fresh truffle and fresh porcini mushrooms two products that can be prohibitively expensive and difficult at best to obtain. Thankfully, Italian canned truffle products and a combination of dry porcini with fresh mushrooms will still yield great results.

INGREDIENTS *4 whole rabbit saddles, bone-in ‖ 6 oz prepared ground truffle ‖ 2 oz dried porcini mushrooms ‖ 6 oz mixed shiitake and crimini mushrooms ‖ 3 cups flour ‖ 3 tablespoons butter ‖ 1 cup extra-virgin olive oil ‖ ⅔ cup carrot, diced ‖ ⅔ cup celery, diced ‖ ⅔ cup onion, diced ‖ 1 bay leaf ‖ 6 fresh sage leaves ‖ 1 sprig thyme ‖ ½ small sprig rosemary ‖ 2 cloves garlic, crushed ‖ ⅔ cup dry white wine ‖ ½ cup dry Marsala ‖ To taste, Kosher salt and fresh ground black pepper*

ONE Use a boning knife to carefully remove the bones from the saddles while still keeping the two loins connected. Once the loin has been detached, remove any bone shards. Reserve the bones and scraps for the sauce. **TWO** Pre-soak the dry porcini in 1½ cups of warm water for 30 minutes. Drain and chop the porcini, reserving the liquid. Chop the mixed mushrooms into small pieces. Heat up ½ cup of the olive oil in a large sauté pan over medium-high heat and cook the mushrooms for 3-4 minutes to soften. Season to taste with salt and pepper. **THREE** Prepare the saddles by seasoning with salt and pepper, and rub a small amount of the prepared truffle on the inside only of each. Similarly apply about ½ of the sautéed chopped mushrooms. Roll the truffle and mushroom tightly into the saddles and secure with butcher's twine. **FOUR** Heat the remaining ½ cup of olive oil in a large skillet. Dredge the rabbit saddles, bones, and scraps into flour and place them into the pan, searing the rabbit on all sides. Add the carrot, celery, onion, garlic, and herbs. Continue to cook over medium heat until the vegetables are cooked. Remove the saddles and finish them in a 350° F oven for 15-20 minutes or until the rabbit is *just* done. Remove and set aside to rest. **FIVE** For the sauce: Mix 2 tablespoons of butter and 2 tablespoons of flour into the same skillet and cook, stirring regularly, for an additional 5-6 minutes to form a roux. Add the white wine and Marsala to the pan along with the reserved porcini water. Simmer, stirring occasionally for 30 minutes. Season with salt and pepper and strain through a fine wire mesh strainer or cheesecloth. Add the remaining truffle and sautéed mushrooms to the sauce. **SIX** Slice the rabbit saddles and serve with the sauce.

Serves 6

PLAYING THE BEARD Cooking at the prestigious *James Beard House* in Manhattan is considered to be the culinary equivalent of a musician playing at *Carnegie Hall*. We "Played the Beard" in 2001 serving this dish (using fresh truffle and fresh porcini) among others.

Grilled veal liver

Americans don't tend to associate liver with Italian cuisine, however Italian cookbooks (up until recently when liver appears to have fallen out of style) show all manner of liver preparations including the classic liver Venetian style, or *Fegato alla Veniziana*, which is basically the same "liver & onions" dish your mother made you growing up. Another specialty of Venice is char-grilled liver, which inspired us to put liver on our menu when we were *Mario's Italian Steakhouse*. Liver isn't for all tastes but liver lovers tell us this is the best liver dish they ever had.

INGREDIENTS *3 lb veal liver, sliced, frozen* ‖ *12 slices applewood bacon* ‖ *2 white onions, sliced* ‖ *¼ cup salad oil* ‖ *½ cup extra-virgin olive oil* ‖ *3 scallions, sliced* ‖ *To taste, Kosher salt and freshly ground pepper* ‖ *6 oz Abruzzi butter (see page 160)*

ONE Heat the salad oil in a skillet over high heat. Add the onions and sauté for several minutes or until they cook throughout and show some browning. **TWO** Place the bacon on a sheet pan and cook at 350° F for 20 minutes or until done to your liking. **THREE** Heat up a gas, charcoal, or oven top grill. Lightly oil both sides of the frozen liver and season to taste with salt and pepper. Because the liver is frozen, it is less likely to stick to the grill and is therefore easier to manipulate. If you do not have frozen liver, it is recommended that you at least partially freeze it. Place the liver on the grill and cook for 2 minutes. Carefully turn it over and cook an additional 2 minutes or until it is done. Slather the cooked liver with Abruzzi butter and top with the onions, bacon, and sliced scallions.

Serves 6

FAQ (NO. 3) What's the difference between veal liver and calves liver? By definition, veal is the meat from a calf that is younger than 12 months old. Liver from milk-fed calves up to the age of 12 months is marketed as "veal liver" where liver from grain fed calves up to the age of 12 months is sold as "calves liver." Veal liver is leaner and lighter in color, and it has much milder and sweeter flavor than calves liver. It's also quite a bit more costly. Hopefully this clears up the confusion.

Veal Mario

The fact we coat the veal with breadcrumbs and serve it with lemons might lead one to conclude that this is our version of the classic Italian Veal *alla Milanese*, but it's not. Our dish *also* calls for a garlic and shallot rub, which flavors the veal. In addition our veal is only lightly dusted with breadcrumbs rather than the more traditional heavy breading method used to prepare Veal *alla Milanese*. We use bone-in veal chops at *Mario's* but veal or even pork cutlets are an excellent substitute.

INGREDIENTS *6 veal chops, about 12 oz each, or 12-18 sliced veal cutlets* ‖ *½ cup extra-virgin olive oil plus ½ cup salad oil, for pan frying* ‖ *⅓ cup extra-virgin olive oil, for the garlic and shallot rub* ‖ *3 cups Italian breadcrumbs* ‖ *2 tablespoons finely chopped garlic* ‖ *2 tablespoons finely chopped shallot* ‖ *1 tablespoon chopped Italian parsley* ‖ *To taste, Kosher salt and freshly ground pepper* ‖ *2 lemons, cut into six wedges each*

ONE Prepare the rub by heating olive oil in a small sauté pan over medium heat. Add the garlic and toast slightly before adding the shallots and parsley. Continue to cook, stirring occasionally, until the shallots are cooked throughout. Set aside to cool. **TWO** Cover the veal chop with plastic wrap and use a meat mallet to pound the veal as thinly as possible, about ¼ inch in thickness. **THREE** Season the veal with salt and pepper and using a pastry brush coat both sides with the garlic and shallot rub, allowing the mixture to adhere to the veal. Dust both sides of the veal lightly with breadcrumbs. **FOUR** Heat a large skillet over medium heat and cover the bottom with a thin ¼ inch layer of the mixed olive and salad oil. When the oil is hot add the veal and sauté for 2-3 minutes before turning over. Continue to cook until the meat is *just* done or cooked to your liking. Remove from the skillet and repeat until all pieces are cooked. Serve with fresh lemon.

Serves 6

BAM, BAM, BAM! If you were to wander through the restaurant on a quiet afternoon chances are, you'll hear the bam, bam, bam, echo of Mario pounding a piece of veal with a meat mallet in preparation for this recipe. A personal favorite and one he loves to prepare for "special guests." We eventually decided to put it on the menu.

Veal scaloppini "pazzo" style

This recipe sprang from the mind of Mario's son Danny who came up with this in an attempt to create a veal dish with all his personal favorite flavors in it. We call it *pazzo*, or crazy style, because no one would be crazy enough to combine these ingredients! No one that is except Danny, who must have been onto something because this dish went on to become a signature menu item both at *Mario's Via Abruzzi* and our other Italian restaurant, *Bazil*.

INGREDIENTS *2½ lb veal cutlet, cut into 18 scallopine style slices ‖ 2 cups flour, for dredging ‖ ¾ cup vegetable oil ‖ 3 oz pancetta, thinly sliced and chopped ‖ 3 oz crimini mushrooms, sliced thin ‖ 3 oz prosciutto, chopped ‖ 1 head escarole, trimmed, chopped, and washed ‖ 9 artichoke hearts, canned ‖ ¾ cup sherry wine ‖ 1 cup veal demi-glace ‖ ½ teaspoon crushed red pepper ‖ 4 tablespoons unsalted butter ‖ To taste, Kosher salt and freshly ground black pepper*

ONE Cover the veal with plastic wrap and use a meat mallet to pound it as thinly as possible, about ¼ inch in thickness. **TWO** Blanch the escarole in boiling water for 1 minute or until tender. **THREE** Heat the oil in a large sauté pan over medium-high heat. Season the veal to taste with salt and pepper before dredging in flour. Shake off any excess flour before adding the veal to the sauté pan. Cook the veal for about 2 minutes or until it becomes golden brown in color. Turn over and continue to cook an additional 2 minutes. Do not overcrowd the pan. Remove the veal from the pan and set aside. **THREE** Add the pancetta to the pan and cook over medium heat for 1 minute before adding the mushrooms. Sauté the mushrooms for 2 minutes or until they are just cooked. **FOUR** Add the veal back to pan along with the prosciutto, escarole, sherry wine, demi-glace, and crushed red pepper. Continue to sauté to heat the ingredients throughout. Season to taste with additional salt and pepper and swirl in the butter to finish.

Serves 6

ANTHONY DANIELE Mario and Flora Daniele's other son is Danny's big brother Anthony. As Owner-slash-General manager at *Mario's* since we opened in 1995, Anthony has led us through many years of change and challenges too numerous to mention. Through it all he never lost his passion for great food and wine, nor his sense of humor! Anthony is also a Monroe County Legislator. He is married to his high-school sweetheart Erin and they live in Pittsford with their three children, Lauren, Michael and Bridget.

Grilled veal tenderloin with shiitake and black truffle

Truffle, or *tartufo*, is one the world's great culinary delicacies. Rare and resistant to cultivation, dogs and occasionally pigs are still trained to find them in season between October and December. Fresh truffles are very pricey and difficult to come by at best but Italian prepared ground truffles are widely available. These products come in various formats including cream of truffle, or *crema di tartufo*, which is packaged in premixed jars or tubes containing various percentages of ground truffle mixed with olives and mushrooms.

INGREDIENTS *2 lb veal tenderloin, cut into 1½-2 inch mignonettes* ‖ *8 oz fresh shiitake mushrooms, sliced* ‖ *3-4 oz Italian-prepared ground truffle* ‖ *½ cup extra-virgin olive oil* ‖ *3 tablespoons shallots, chopped* ‖ *1 tablespoon garlic, finely chopped* ‖ *3 tablespoons Italian parsley, chopped* ‖ *To taste, Kosher salt and freshly ground pepper*

ONE Pre-heat a gas, charcoal or stove top grill. Season the veal mignonettes with salt and pepper and brush with olive oil. Grill to your preferred doneness. If you do not have access to a grill, pan sear the veal over high heat in a skillet on the stove. **TWO** Heat the olive oil in a large sauté pan over medium-high heat. Add the chopped garlic and fry until the garlic begins to turn a golden color. Add the shallots and parsley and cook 2 minutes or until the shallots soften. Add the mushrooms and cook 3-4 minutes until the mushrooms are cooked throughout. Season to taste with salt and pepper. **THREE** Add the prepared truffle to the mushroom mixture. Cook for 30 additional seconds and serve over the veal. We like to serve this dish with mashed potatoes and sautéed spinach as shown in the photo.

Serves 6

FAQ (NO. 4) Why did you take *that* off the menu? First, we apologize to all of you whose favorite menu item is no longer available at *Mario's*. However please note: if all we did was add new items to our menu it would eventually become far too large to execute so inevitably something must to go. Unfortunately there are always customers who are disappointed by the sudden disappearance of their favorite menu item. Usually the first ones to go are those that are not selling well but sometimes it's a matter of the menu mix. We have to maintain a balanced menu so sometimes even the best dishes have to make way for something new.

Osso bucco all' Abruzzese

We offered this Abruzzese style braised veal shank every Sunday for several years as one of the rotating weekly specials that were featured on the menu. It is the atypical addition of porcini and tomato to the braising liquid that makes this Abruzzi style. We serve this dish with saffron risotto.

INGREDIENTS *12 veal shanks, cut 2 inches thick ‖ 3 cups all-purpose flour ‖ 1 cup vegetable oil ‖ ½ cup extra-virgin olive oil ‖ 2 bay leaves ‖ 1 sprig rosemary ‖ 5 cloves garlic, sliced ‖ 3 cups carrots, diced ‖ 3 cups celery, diced ‖ 3 cups onions, diced ‖ 2 oz dried porcini mushrooms ‖ 1 can (35 oz) whole peeled tomatoes ‖ 1 bottle dry white wine ‖ Water as needed to cover ‖ To taste, Kosher salt and freshly ground pepper ‖ 2 cloves garlic, 1 sprig Italian parsley and the zest of one lemon, chopped, for gremoulata*

SAFFRON RISOTTO *2½ cup Arborio rice ‖ 1 teaspoon saffron threads ‖ ½ cup onion, finely chopped ‖ ½ cup extra-virgin olive oil ‖ ¾ cup dry white wine ‖ 6 cups water or homemade chicken broth (see page 61) or use canned chicken broth ‖ ½ cup parmigiano-reggiano or grana-padana cheese, freshly grated ‖ 3 tablespoons unsalted butter ‖ To taste, Kosher salt and freshly ground pepper*

ONE Heat the oil in a large braising pan over moderate heat. Adjust the quantity as needed so the oil is about ½ inches deep. Season the veal shanks with salt and pepper and dredge them in flour. Place the shanks topside down in the skillet for several minutes before rotating them on all sides to brown. Remove the shanks from the pan and set aside. Drain the cooking oil from the pan, taking care to retain the pan drippings and caramelized bits. **TWO** Return the pan to the stove and add the olive oil, carrot, onion, celery, garlic, bay leaf, and rosemary. Sauté 5-6 minutes to soften the vegetables. Add the veal shanks, white wine, porcini mushrooms and tomatoes, breaking the tomatoes up as you go. Add water or chicken stock to *just* cover the veal shanks. Cover the pan with a vented lid or foil and simmer over low heat for 2 hours or until the shanks are tender. **THREE** To prepare the saffron risotto: Heat the olive oil in a saucepan over medium-high heat, add the onion, and sauté until soft. Add the rice and saffron. Stir until the grains are well coated with oil. Add the wine and stir briefly. Add enough of the water or broth to cover the rice completely and simmer gently over low heat until most of the liquid is absorbed. Continue to add the liquid in this way until the rice is cooked. Stir in the cheese and butter and season to taste with salt and pepper. Serve promptly. **FOUR** Serve the osso bucco with the risotto and some of the pan the sauce.

Serves 6

FIELDS OF GOLD Fields of saffron crocus, the flower from which saffron is harvested, can be seen from Mario's mother Esilde's house in Castelnuovo, Abruzzi.

Grilled pork loin with olive-raisin sauce

We were pleasantly surprised by how well received this dish was when we had it on the menu. After all who mixes olives with raisins? This recipe calls for olive paste, if you have trouble finding it you can grind pitted kalamata olives with a little olive oil in your food processor instead.

INGREDIENTS *6 boneless pork loin chops, 10-12 ounces each ‖ 3 tablespoons extra-virgin olive oil ‖ 2 cups veal demi-glace, available in most grocery stores ‖ ½ cup brandy ‖ ½ cup raisins ‖ 2 tablespoons black olive paste ‖ ½ sprig fresh rosemary ‖ 1-2 tablespoons table sugar or to taste ‖ To taste, Kosher salt and freshly ground pepper*

ONE Roughly chop the raisins and put them in a container with about 2 tablespoons of brandy. Allow the raisins to absorb some of the brandy for about 1-2 hours while cooking. **TWO** Add the demi-glace to a small saucepot with the rosemary and remaining brandy. Cook over medium-high heat to reduce the volume and until the liquid thickens to a sauce consistency. **THREE** Remove the rosemary sprig and add the raisins, olive paste, sugar, and season to taste with sea salt and freshly ground pepper to finish the sauce. **FOUR** Season the pork to taste with salt and pepper. Lightly coat the pork with oil before pan searing or oven-broiling. The pork will be done when the center temperature has reached 160° F. Serve the pork with the sauce.

Serves 6

ROBERTO DONNA We became acquainted with celebrated Italian Chef Roberto Donna through our affiliation with *Gruppo Ristoratori Italiano* (GRI) a non-profit organization, involving member restaurants engaged in the promotion of Italian cuisine and culture in North America. We cooked for several GRI events in both Washington, DC and New York and Roberto let us hang out for several days in the kitchen at his flagship restaurant *Galileo* in Washington as part of our GRI experience. Suffice it to say we took a lot of careful notes. The idea for this recipe came from Roberto on one of those trips.

Pork chops braised in cream with onions, thyme and rosemary

Maiale alla latte, or pork braised in milk, is a centuries old dish originating in Central Italy. In our version fresh cream is used instead of milk, and we add lots of onions and sprigs of rosemary and thyme to give the sauce more substance and additional flavor. Traditionalists will note that it's not quite the same but we think by adding the cream the resulting sauce is thicker, richer and arguably more flavorful. The pork and the cream are transformed as they slowly cook together with the onions, thyme and rosemary.

INGREDIENTS *8-10 pork chops ‖ ¾ cup salad oil ‖ 2 oz unsalted butter ‖ 2 onions, sliced ‖ 4 cups heavy cream ‖ 1 sprig rosemary, stripped from the stem ‖ 1-2 sprigs thyme, stripped from the stem ‖ To taste, Kosher salt and freshly ground pepper*

ONE Heat the oil over medium heat in a large heavy-bottomed skillet. Season the chops to taste with salt and pepper and place them in the pan. Sear them on one side for about 1-2 minutes to brown them before turning them over and browning the other side. **TWO** Drain the oils, taking care to retain the pork drippings and add the onions, thyme, rosemary and heavy cream. Simmer over low heat until the pork is cooked throughout and the onions are tender. Use a meat thermometer to check for doneness. The pork will be done when the center temperature has reached 160° F. **THREE** Remove the pork and onions using a slotted spoon and bring the remaining sauce to a boil over medium-high heat. Once it begins to boil, evaporation will take place and the cream will reduce in

volume and begin to thicken. Once thickened to a sauce-like consistency, season to taste with salt and pepper. Add the pork and onions back to the skillet and warm throughout before serving.

Serves 6

FOODIES ON A BUDGET TAKE NOTE With beef and lamb prices at all time highs and fish prices surpassing red meat prices for the first time in history, pork remains an affordable protein option. This dish gives the foodie-on-a-budget an opportunity to serve an outstanding authentic Italian meal that is affordable without sacrificing quality. Risotto or a simple parmigiano mashed potato and sautéed greens like spinach, Swiss chard or broccoli rape, are excellent accompaniments to this dish.

Porchetta

Porcetta is a traditional street food of Central Italy. It is a simple pork dish but there is a special flavor that is the result of careful attention to preparation and also from the fact that traditionally a whole pig is roasted. Even at *Mario's* we don't have an oven big enough to cook something that big so we developed our own porchetta recipe using bone-in, skin-on fresh pork hams. These give comparable results because it's like roasting *part* of a whole pig. In keeping with Abruzzese tradition this recipe was written to accommodate a larger gathering. We serve this every Sunday on our brunch buffet.

INGREDIENTS *1 fresh ham, bone-in and skin-on ‖ 1 cup fresh rosemary, chopped ‖ 20 bay leaves ‖ ½ cup garlic, chopped or sliced ‖ 2 cups white wine ‖ 1 cup Kosher salt ‖ ¼ cup freshly ground black pepper ‖ As needed, butcher's twine or kitchen string*

ONE Carefully remove the bone from the pork, cutting the meat back around the bone. The best approach is from the backside (the side opposite the skin). Once the bone is removed, lay the pork out, cutting the thicker parts back so you have a slab of more-or-less equal thickness. **TWO** Season the inside liberally with salt and pepper and rub the rosemary, bay leaf, and garlic into the pork. Douse with white wine. Allow the pork to rest, or cure, in the refrigerator overnight if possible and save a small amount of your seasonings so they can be applied the following day. **THREE** The following day, re-season the pork with salt and pepper, making sure to season the outside skin liberally. Roll the pork lengthwise into a roll and secure it tightly with kitchen string or butcher's twine. Drizzle white wine onto the skin and puncture in several places with a small knife. This important step will allow steam to escape as the meat cooks, allowing the pork to roast rather than steam in its own juice. **FOUR** Roast at 250° F for 2 ½-3 hours then turn the oven up to 400° F for an additional 30 minutes. The juices should run clear when the meat is punctured and the skin should be crisp. If additional cooking is required, turn the oven back down to 250° F. Serve either warm or at room temperature.

Makes 1 porchetta

GIMME SOME SKIN! (NO. 2) In Italy, the crispy pork skin on the outside of the porchetta is considered to be a delicacy, so we always break it off and leave it on the carving board at brunch. Rarely does it go uneaten!

Grilled baby lamb chops

Italy is a pastoral land and Italians have been shepherding lamb since antiquity. Together with pork, lamb continues to be the meat the cuisine is centered around. Out of the hundreds of dishes that have been on our various menus over the years, this one has always been there, remaining virtually unchanged since *Mario's* opened in 1995. To not have grilled lamb on our menu would be unthinkable.

INGREDIENTS *4 New Zealand baby lamb racks, Frenched ‖ 3 cups panko (Japanese) breadcrumbs ‖ 1 teaspoon, chopped rosemary ‖ 3 bay leaves, well crumbled ‖ 1 cup extra-virgin olive oil ‖ To taste, Kosher salt and freshly ground black pepper ‖ 1 lemon cut into wedges*

ONE Process panko style breadcrumbs in a food processor until they are finely textured. Season them with salt and pepper to taste and combine with ½ cup of olive oil. **TWO** Cut the lamb racks into chops and season with salt and pepper to taste. Make a marinade by combining the olive oil, garlic, rosemary, and bay leaf and coat the chops with it. Allow the chops to marinate at least 1-2 hours. Dredge the marinated chops in the breadcrumbs to coat them evenly on both sides. **THREE** Pre-heat a char broiler. Grill the chops for about 2 minutes per side or until done to your preference. The chops can also be oven-roasted or pan-fried if you do not have access to a grill. Serve the lamb with fresh lemon and good quality olive oil for drizzling.

Serves 6

FAQ (NO. 5) Why Baby New Zealand and not domestic lamb? Italians prefer milk-fed baby lamb, or *abbachio*, which is highly touted in Italy for its lean, tender and delicately flavored meat. At Mario's our chops come from Baby New Zealand lamb because they are milder, leaner and tenderer than chops cut from domestic lamb, which makes them more like *abbachio*.

Roasted leg of lamb

Leg of lamb is a brunch staple that we serve every Sunday on our brunch buffet. Preparing lamb this way and carving it tableside is perfect for a big Sunday night family dinner or on special occasions and holidays. The important thing is to trim away as much of the fat as possible. Trimming the fat will give you a more delicate and sweeter meat that will be much less gamey than it would otherwise be. Besides, this is the way it's done in Italy, so that's how we do it at *Mario's*.

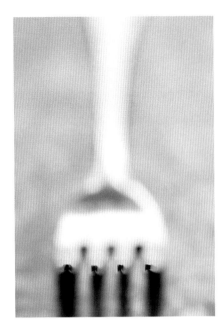

INGREDIENTS *6-7 lb boneless leg of lamb, or a whole bone-in leg of lamb ‖ ½ cup extra-virgin olive oil ‖ 2 sprigs fresh rosemary ‖ 3 bay leaves ‖ 4 whole garlic cloves, split ‖ 1 tablespoon chopped garlic ‖ 3 tablespoons Kosher salt ‖ ½ tablespoon freshly ground black pepper*

ONE Unwrap and rinse the leg. If the leg is boneless and netted, remove the net. Trim away as much excess fat as possible. Tie up the leg with butcher's twine by circling the meat with three lengths of twine, pulling the string tightly, and typing a knot. If you are using a bone-in leg of lamb, tying will not be necessary. **TWO** Using a utility knife poke 8 holes in several places around the leg. Insert half a clove of garlic, a bit of rosemary, and bay leaf into each hole. Crumble the remaining bay leaf and chop the remaining rosemary. Combine these with olive oil and chopped garlic. Coat the leg with this mixture. Season generously on all sides with salt and pepper. **THREE** Roast the lamb at 350° F to your preferred doneness. In Italy, lamb is nearly always cooked to 150° F or medium-medium well.

Serves 10

THE BIG, BIG BRUNCH The recipes in this book for roasted leg of lamb, porchetta, and roasted salmon with herb sauce all come from our Sunday brunch repertoire. Our brunch recipe file includes over 300 separate dishes with nearly 200 antipasti and salad recipes. Perhaps our next book should be titled "Mario's 100 Best Brunch Recipes."

Mario's char-grilled steak with Abruzzi butter

At the restaurant we use a 1600° F char-grill to cook our steaks. The intense heat sears the meat for that nice char-grilled flavor and seals in the juices, which is how a steak should be done. Save this recipe for a summer evening when you can use your gas or charcoal grill. Keep the lid on your grill until the last minute for maximum heat before putting on the steaks. We dress our steaks with Abruzzi butter, which is as important to the popularity of our steaks as the cooking method.

When picking out steaks choose those graded USDA choice or higher and note that not all steaks of the same grade are created equal, so be sure to examine them for marbling. Marbling is the visible streaks of creamy white fat found within the meat itself. Well-marbled steaks are less tough and they have better flavor. Avoid steaks that have little or no visible marbling.

INGREDIENTS *6 steaks of any cut* ‖ *2 tablespoons extra-virgin olive oil* ‖ *To taste, Kosher salt and freshly ground pepper*

ABRUZZI BUTTER *8 oz unsalted butter* ‖ *2 tablespoons garlic, chopped* ‖ *2 tablespoons shallots, chopped* ‖ *½ cup fresh, chopped basil* ‖ *To taste, Kosher salt and freshly ground pepper*

ONE For the Abruzzi butter: Heat the oil in a sauté pan and lightly toast the garlic. Add the shallots and cook until they soften. Combine the butter, salt, and pepper in a mixing bowl. Add the garlic and shallots and whip for 2 minutes on high speed to incorporate air into the butter. Add the basil and mix to combine. Do not over mix after adding the basil. Keep the butter at room temperature. **TWO** Preheat the grill, cover on, for 15-20 minutes. Brush the steaks with olive oil and season to taste with salt and pepper. Open the grill and brush it down with a wire grill brush before quickly putting the steaks on. Grill to the desired degree of doneness. **THREE** Slather the steak generously with the butter and serve promptly.

Serves 6

THE STEAKHOUSE YEARS In 2007 *Mario's Via Abruzzi* officially became *Mario's Italian Steakhouse and Catering*. Why the change? The simple answer is-we wanted to more clearly differentiate *Mario's* and *Bazil*, our other Italian restaurant and since steaks were already selling well at *Mario's* the change seemed like a natural progression. Besides we love a good steak! We decided to re-focus our attention on Italian food, which explains why we dropped the "*Italian Steakhouse*" part of the name in 2009 and are now just *Mario's* but steaks are still featured prominently on our menu.

Meatballs

These are Mario's meatballs, just the way the boss has been making them for years. At the restaurant we make them big, half-pounders to be exact, but you can make them any size you wish. This is one of our most requested recipes and now anyone can make them. We like to serve them with Mario's pasta sauce, with or without pasta. They also make an awesome meatball sandwich.

INGREDIENTS *1½ lb ground beef, 80% lean* ‖ *1½ lb ground pork* ‖ *¾ cup whole milk* ‖ *3 large eggs* ‖ *2 tablespoons Italian parsley, chopped* ‖ *12-14 ounces panko (Japanese) breadcrumbs* ‖ *5 oz grana-padana or parmigiano-reggiano cheese, grated* ‖ *1½ teaspoon chopped garlic* ‖ *To taste, Kosher salt and freshly ground pepper* ‖ *½ cup extra-virgin olive oil and ½ cup salad oil, mixed, for frying* ‖ *1 batch Mario's marinara (see page 2) or use 2 jars Mario's Pasta Sauce*

ONE In a large bowl, combine the ground beef, ground pork, parmesan, parsley, garlic, salt, pepper, and olive oil. Mix to combine. Add the egg, milk, and breadcrumbs and *gently* mix to combine. **TWO** Roll lightly into roughly six 8-ounce balls or divide into whatever portion size you prefer. **THREE** Heat the oils over medium heat in a large skillet (preferably Teflon-coated). You should have about ⅓ inch of oil in the bottom of the skillet that will then rise up to about ½ inch once the meatballs are added. Brown the meatballs on all sides for several minutes to obtain a nice brown color. The meatballs should be about halfway cooked at this point. Drain the oil off and cover with Mario's Pasta Sauce. Add 1 cup of water to loosen. Simmer slowly over very low heat until cooked throughout. Alternatively, transfer the halfway cooked meatballs to a 350 °F oven and cook for 15-20 minutes or as needed to cook throughout. Serve with Mario's pasta sauce.

Makes 6 8-ounce meatballs

MARIO'S PASTA SAUCES In 2003 we supplied *LiDestri Foods* in Fairport, NY with a recipe and a sample of our Marinara Sauce to see if they could duplicate it. After several trial batches they were finally able to reproduce it to perfection and in 2004 we started marketing it locally as Mario's Pasta Sauce. The sauce is now being sold in 1,500 supermarkets throughout our regional area and beyond including *Wegmans* where it is the top selling sauce in its price (mid-priced) range. In 2006 we added Vodka Sauce and Three Cheese Marinara to our sauce line. It's a point of pride for all of us that it has been such a huge success.

Specialta di Mare—
fish and seafood

Top Left, Danny and Mario Daniele 1978;
Bottom Left, Danny, Anthony and Flora Daniele 1978;
Middle, Mario Daniele with his first (and only) boss;
Top Right, Flora, Gabriella, Francesco and Regina Gasbarre 1948;
Bottom Right, Danny and Anthony Daniele 1979

Brodetto

Brodetto is the *zuppa di pesce* of the Abruzzi region. Like other Italian seafood in broth dishes, plenty of garlic, hot peppers and tomatoes are used but it's the addition of sweet peppers that make it Abruzzese. Some other regional variations include the addition of the local saffron or a touch of vinegar. The seafood we use are somewhat different from what you would find in Italy, where they emphasize finfish more than shellfish, but the resultant flavor is authentic Abruzzi. This was one of our staple menu items for many years.

INGREDIENTS *3 lobsters, 1½ lb each, cut in half ‖ 18 jumbo shrimp, peeled and de-veined ‖ 18 sea scallops ‖ 18 littleneck clams, cleaned ‖ 18 cockle clams, cleaned ‖ 18 black mussels, cleaned ‖ 1½ lb fresh swordfish or tuna, sliced into 6 pieces ‖ 1½ lb squid, cleaned with tubes and cut into rings ‖ 6 cups plum tomatoes, peeled, seeded, and diced ‖ 3 cups tomato juice ‖ 3 cups clam juice ‖ 3 cups extra-virgin olive oil ‖ ½ cup fresh garlic, chopped ‖ 3 cups onion, diced ‖ 3 cups green bell pepper, diced ‖ 3 anchovies, smashed ‖ 1½ cup white wine, dry ‖ 1 packed cup fresh basil leaves, torn or chopped ‖ 3 bay leaves ‖ ½ cup fresh Italian parsley, chopped ‖ To taste, crushed red pepper or dried hot pepper pods ‖ To taste, sea salt and freshly ground black pepper*

ONE Heat the oil in a large skillet or paella pan and add the lobster, swordfish, and littleneck clams. Cook for 3 minutes. Add garlic, bay leaf, parsley, and hot peppers to taste. Cook 2-3 minutes or until the garlic turns golden brown. Add the clam and tomato juices. Cover and simmer until the clams open. Discard any clams that do not open or have an off odor.

TWO Add the tomatoes, basil, bell peppers, onions, anchovy, cockle clams, mussels, shrimp, calamari, and scallops. Cover and cook down until all the fish are cooked and begin to absorb the color of the liquid. Season with salt and pepper to taste.

THREE To serve individually: Take out the lobsters and swordfish and place them into 6 large bowls. Then put 3 shrimp and 3 scallops into the bowls and carefully portion the clams and mussels. Pour the remaining broth ingredients over the seafood and garnish with chopped parsley and a parsley sprig. We like to serve this with grilled slices of Italian bread.

Serves 6

PREPARING FOR SIX You may be looking at this recipe and wondering how you can possibly pull it off for six people with all these ingredients (including three whole lobsters) in one pot! Our recommendation? Use a large paella pan.

Haddock with tomatoes, onions and basil

Haddock is a hugely popular fish in Rochester, NY and surrounding areas where a Friday night "fish-fry," consisting of beer battered haddock with tartar sauce, French fries and coleslaw, is a weekly ritual for many people. Of course deep-fried fish is not on the menu for those watching their waistlines and cholesterol levels. This recipe is a great option if you're craving something besides the typical "broiled" haddock that is usually offered at fish-fry restaurants.

INGREDIENTS *6 fresh haddock filets, 10-12 ounce each* ‖ *2 lb plum (Roma) tomatoes* ‖ *1 cup onion, chopped* ‖ *1 cup extra-virgin olive oil* ‖ *1 cup clam juice* ‖ *⅔ cup basil, chopped* ‖ *1 tablespoon parsley, chopped* ‖ *To taste, Sea salt and freshly ground black pepper*

ONE Using a paring knife, cut a small x in the top of the tomatoes. Submerge them in boiling water for about 1 minute or until the skins begin to blister. Remove and cool them in ice water. Peel and cut in half. Gently squeeze out the seeds and chop. **TWO** Place the fish skin side down into 1 or 2 baking dishes as needed. Season with salt and pepper to taste. Disperse the onions and tomatoes evenly over the fish. Add the basil and chopped parsley. Finally, add the clam juice and extra-virgin olive oil and season to taste with salt and pepper. **THREE** Cover with aluminum foil and bake at 350° F for 15 minutes or until the fish and tomatoes are just cooked. Serve the haddock topped with the tomatoes.

Serves 6

MARIO'S FISH FRY For decades we served classic Rochester style fish-fries on Friday nights at *Mario's Pizza & Pasta* on East Avenue. When *Mario's Via Abruzzi* opened we opted to offer a mixed fish fry or *fritura misto di mare* instead. This consisted of haddock, shrimp, scallops and calamari dipped in a light egg white and flour batter as one might prepare it in Italy. At one point we tried doing a traditional Rochester style fish fry but our clientele clamored for us to bring back the *fritura misto* instead.

Roasted salmon with lobster-artichoke ragù

The concept here is simple and it all revolves around the lobster. We start by splitting the three lobsters down the middle and carefully removing the tails. These will be roasted with the salmon. The remaining lobster claw and knuckle meat will go into the ragout and the leftover shells will get cooked down with aromatic vegetables and fresh cream to make the sauce. This dish was created at *Mario's*.

INGREDIENTS *3 whole live lobsters, 1¼ pound each* ‖ *2-2½ lb salmon, cut into 6 equally-sized portions* ‖ *1 quart heavy (whipping) cream* ‖ *½ cup extra-virgin olive oil* ‖ *2 cups onion, chopped* ‖ *2 cups celery, chopped* ‖ *1 cup carrot, chopped* ‖ *1 small sprig fresh thyme* ‖ *8-10 leaves fresh sage* ‖ *1 small sprig fresh rosemary* ‖ *3 fresh artichokes or use canned artichokes* ‖ *1 lemon* ‖ *To taste, sea salt and freshly ground pepper*

ONE Remove and trim back the tough outer leaves from the artichokes and remove the choke. Boil for 6-7 minutes, or until tender, in water that has been acidified with the juice of one lemon. Strain and set aside to cool before cutting into wedges. If using canned whole artichokes, carefully rinse them and cut into wedges. **TWO** Remove the tail and claws from the lobster. Cut the tails in half lengthwise. The remaining lobster bodies and shells will be used to make the sauce and the split tails and claws will be roasted with the salmon. **THREE** Heat a large braising pan over medium-high heat, add the olive oil, the remaining shells, fresh herbs, carrot and about half the onion and celery. Sauté for 10 minutes. Add the heavy cream and boil over high heat to cook down cream by about half or until the cream thickens and takes on a distinct shine. Strain the cream through a fine wire strainer or cheesecloth and season to taste with salt and pepper. **FOUR** Sauté the remaining onion and celery in oil until the vegetables soften. Add the pre-cooked artichoke and the lobster cream base sauce to this mixture and bring to simmer. **FIVE** Lay the cut salmon, lobster tails and claws onto a sheet pan, brush with extra-virgin olive oil and season with salt and pepper. Roast in the oven at 350° F for 8-10 minutes or until just cooked. Remove the lobster meat from the claws and add it to the cream sauce to complete the ragout. **SIX** For presentation stack the salmon and lobster on sautéed spinach or other dark green leafy vegetable and carefully spoon over some of the lobster-artichoke ragù.

Serves 6

CARMINE'S TABLE Carmine Sprio had a regionally popular syndicated cooking show called *Carmine's Table* that ran for several years on the Fox network. The show was filmed in the studio kitchen at his now defunct restaurant *Carmine's* in Albany, NY. We did a full half-hour episode with the ever-positive and positively charming Carmine in 2002 where we presented this dish.

Roasted salmon with fresh herb sauce

Possessing a truly unique flavor (Does any other fish taste like salmon?) and great health benefits (it's very high in omega-3 fatty acids that contribute to cardiovascular health) salmon has always been the most popular fish on our menus. The question "What can I do with salmon at home?" is one that comes up often and here is *the* answer, a dish that easy to prepare, flavorful and healthy too! What makes this recipe special is the fresh herb sauce. This bright tasting fresh herb concoction was created at *Mario's*.

INGREDIENTS *6 salmon filets, 6-8 oz each or one 2-3 lb side of salmon that you can serve whole ‖ ¼ cup extra-virgin olive oil ‖ To taste, sea salt and freshly ground pepper ‖ 2 lemons, cut into wedges*

FRESH HERB SAUCE *½ cup fresh basil, finely chopped ‖ ½ cup fresh parsley, finely chopped ‖ ¼ cup fresh rosemary, finely chopped ‖ ¼ cup fresh sage, finely chopped ‖ 1 teaspoon fresh thyme, picked from the stem ‖ 1 teaspoon garlic, finely chopped ‖ ⅔ cup extra-virgin oil ‖ To taste, Kosher or sea salt and freshly ground pepper*

ONE Place the salmon filets or whole salmon onto a suitably sized sheet pan. Drizzle the olive oil over the salmon and season to taste with salt and pepper. Roast in a preheated 350° F oven for 15-20 minutes or until the fish is just done. **TWO** To make the fresh herb sauce: Combine all the herbs in a bowl, season with salt and pepper to taste and serve. **THREE** Brush, drizzle, or rub some of the herb sauce onto the fish and serve. Serve with additional sauce and fresh lemon wedges.

Serves 6

MARIO'S HERB SAUCE Our herb sauce is an all-purpose condiment that will keep for 2-3 weeks in the refrigerator. It's also excellent on steaks and lamb chops and even grilled vegetables. For a creamy variation try mixing it with mayonnaise or adding it to a cream reduction for an herb cream sauce. Feel free to substitute and vary the herbs to your own taste.

Tilapia *carpione*

Carpione is a sugar and vinegar based condiment that is flavored with aromatic vegetables and herbs. It has been around since the Middle Ages when it was used as a method of fish preservation. You can still find *carpione* in most grocery stores in Italy, where small fish, usually anchovies, are preserved in glass jars often labeled sweet-and-sour, or *agro dolce*. Here we use lots of thinly sliced onion, simmered in sweetened vinegar and flavored with rosemary, hot peppers, bay leaf and garlic. This sauce provides a bright sweet, sour & spicy counter point to the mild flavored tilapia.

INGREDIENTS *6 tilapia filets, about 2 lb ‖ 6 large eggs ‖ 1¼ cup extra-virgin olive oil ‖ 2 cups all-purpose flour ‖ 2 large onions, thinly sliced ‖ 4-6 fresh garlic cloves ‖ ⅔ cup white wine vinegar ‖ 2 tablespoons sugar ‖ 1 sprig fresh rosemary ‖ 2 bay leaves ‖ 6 hot pepper pods, or to taste, crushed red pepper ‖ To taste, sea salt and freshly ground pepper*

ONE Heat about ¾ cup of the olive oil in a saucepan over medium heat. Add the onion, garlic, rosemary, bay leaf, and pepper pods. Sauté until the onions soften and are *just* cooked. Take care not to brown or caramelize the onions, turning down the heat as needed. Add the vinegar and bring to a simmer for several minutes to allow the flavors to develop. Remove from the heat and season to taste with salt. **TWO** Whisk the eggs and season to taste with salt and pepper. **THREE** Heat the oil in a large sauté pan over moderate heat. Season the fish filets with salt and pepper before coating them with flour. Shake off the excess flour and dip them into the egg. Quickly transfer the fish to the sauté pan and cook for 3 minutes to set the egg and obtain and nice color. Turn the fish over and sauté over low heat for 3-4 more minutes or until cooked throughout. Cooking time will depending upon the size of the fish filets. Remove the fish from the pan and top with the onion mixture.

Serves 6

SUSTAINABLE SEAFOOD In recent years sustainability has become a food service industry buzzword. Fish populations in particular are being threatened by increasing demand and continued over fishing. More and more, restaurants and seafood providers are looking for organizations like the *Marine Stewardship Council* and others to aid them in purchasing sustainable seafood. Tilapia are farm-raised and thus considered sustainable; as an added bonus to the consumer, they are a healthy choice that's also very affordable.

Monkfish with tomatoes, saffron, and crazy water

In Italy they mostly serve the local catch so you are much more likely to see a fish like monkfish on the menu than say salmon, haddock or swordfish. At *Ristorante Beccaceci* in Guliananova, they serve this monkfish dish, which makes use of crazy water, or *aqua pazzo*, the natural juice that is given off by freshly chopped tomatoes.

INGREDIENTS *6 fresh monkfish filets, about 3 lb, or other of firm-fleshed white fish ‖ 2 lb plum (Roma) tomatoes ‖ 1 cup onion, finely chopped ‖ 1 cup extra-virgin olive oil ‖ 1 cup grana-padana or parmigiano-reggiano cheese, grated ‖ 3 pinches saffron threads ‖ To taste, Kosher salt and freshly ground pepper*

ONE Using a knife score the tomatoes with an x on the top. Place them in boiling water for 30 seconds or until the skin begins to loosen. Peel off the skins and then cut the tomatoes in half. Place a wire mesh strainer over a bowl and gently squeeze out the seeds and juice into it. Empty the seeds from the strainer. Chop the tomatoes and place them into the strainer to collect the additional juice the tomatoes will yield. It is best to do this one-hour before cooking so the tomatoes will have time to drain. **TWO** Add about 1 cup of the crazy water to a small saucepan. Add the saffron and bring to a brief simmer. You want to retain the freshness of the tomato juice so all you want to do is heat the crazy water enough for the saffron flavor to be released. **THREE** Remove the connective tissue and dark tinted areas on the outside of the fish. Heat the extra-virgin olive oil in a large non-stick sauté pan. Season the fish to taste with salt and pepper. Place them into the skillet to pan-sear. Turn the fish as needed to sear on all sides and cook until the filets are *just* done. Remove the fish from the pan and set aside. Add the onion to the pan and sauté for 2 minutes or until softened. Add the tomatoes and sauté until they are cooked throughout. Add the saffron-tomato juice and season to taste with salt and pepper. **FOUR** Return the fish to the pan and cook for 1 minute, allowing the fish to absorb the flavors and golden color of the saffron. Remove the fish to serve. Add half of the cheese to the sauce and toss to incorporate. Pour the sauce over the fish and garnish with the remaining cheese.

Serves 6

NO CHEESE PLEASE! The addition of cheese to fish is normally a culinary no-no in Italy, because Italians feel that cheese overwhelms the delicate taste of fish. This modern Abruzzese recipe, which calls for grated grana-padana or parmigiano-reggiano cheese, makes an exception to the general rule.

Sea bass and shrimp wrapped in zucchini

Like other cold-water species, Chilean sea bass is rich and buttery. It's ideal for this recipe because the fish takes on the essence of the shrimp as the two cook together. The concept here is to sandwich the shrimp between two layers of fish and wrap the whole thing with strips of zucchini, yellow squash and carrot. This elegant dish can be prepared ahead of time and baked before serving. It is served with a simple cream reduction that is flavored with fresh lemon.

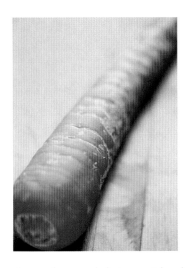

INGREDIENTS *6 Chilean sea bass filets, 2½-3 lb ‖ 1 lb shrimp, peeled and de-veined ‖ 2 zucchini ‖ 2 yellow squash ‖ 2 carrots, the same size as the squash ‖ 2-3 cups panko (Japanese) breadcrumbs ‖ 1 cup extra-virgin olive oil ‖ To taste, sea salt and freshly ground black pepper*

LEMON CREAM SAUCE *4 cups heavy cream ‖ 1 cup white wine ‖ 1 shallot ‖ 1 lemon, juiced ‖ ½ bay leaf ‖ 12 chives ‖ To taste, Kosher salt and white pepper*

ONE. Prepare the individual sea bass filets so you can sandwich the shrimp inside the bass. **TWO** Peel the carrots and blanch them for 4-5 minutes in boiling water or as needed to soften. Then, using a vegetable mandoline, slice the squash and carrots lengthwise into thin strips. The vegetables should be just thin enough to wrap around the fish without breaking (see page 41). **THREE** Season the sea bass and shrimp with salt and pepper and toss them in the olive oil to coat. Add the breadcrumbs and toss to generously coat. Divide the shrimp into 6 portions and sandwich a portion of the shrimp inside the fish. Fold the strips of zucchini, yellow squash, and carrot in a parallel, slightly overlapping fashion around the fish, making sure the vegetables are tucked underneath. Dust with more breadcrumbs and drizzle some additional extra-virgin olive oil as needed. **FOUR** For the lemon cream sauce: Boil the wine in a saucepan with the shallot and bay leaf until you have about ⅓ cup of wine left. In a separate thick-bottomed or non-stick skillet, boil the cream and cook it down until it thickens and takes on a distinct shine. Strain the wine into the cream and continue to cook down to obtain a sauce consistency. Add the lemon juice, strain and season with salt and white pepper to taste. **FIVE** Bake the fish at 325° F for 25 minutes or until cooked throughout. Cut in half and serve on a pool of the sauce.

Serves 6

WHITE GOLD Patagonian Toothfish, also known as Chilean Sea Bass, are highly prized white fish that have been dubbed "white gold" by the fishing industry. Sadly, sustainability initiatives and moratoriums designed to protect these fish are often ignored and thousands of tons of Chilean Sea Bass are sold illegally through the black market.

Roasted whole Dover sole

In Italy the traditional method for roasting fish is in a hinged wire rack, similar to what you might find among the accessories next to the gas grills at the local home improvement store. The rack is closed securing the fish (which are coated in oiled breadcrumbs) and then thrust into a big furnace-like oven specifically designed for this purpose. The end result is slightly charred on the outside, moist and perfectly cooked on the inside. We simulate what they do in Italy by first placing the fish on our char-broiler to obtain grill marks. We then finish it in the oven on a standard wire rack (to allow the air to circulate), mimicking the hinged wire rack used in Italy.

INGREDIENTS *6 whole Dover soles, or the equivalent fresh sole filets ‖ 6 cups plain breadcrumbs ‖ 1½ cup extra-virgin olive oil for the breadcrumbs ‖ To taste, Kosher salt and freshly ground black pepper ‖ 2 tablespoons Italian parsley, chopped ‖ 2 lemons cut into six wedges ‖ ½ cup extra-virgin olive oil, for drizzling*

ONE Combine the breadcrumbs with the olive oil and season with salt and pepper to taste. **TWO** Remove the skin by starting at the tail end of the fish and pulling away the skin. Lightly rub oil onto the fish and season with salt and pepper. Dredge the fish in the breadcrumbs so that it is generously and evenly coated. **THREE** Preheat the char-broiler on high heat. Place the sole directly onto the grill. Turn over when the fish has begun to char on one side. Grill to obtain char marks on the other side. **FOUR** Transfer to large baking pans. If possible, put wire baking or cooling racks in the pans to allow the fish to sit above the pan so the heat circulates evenly around the fish. Place in a preheated 350° F oven for 15-20 minutes or until the fish is *just* done. Present the fish on a plate dressed with extra-virgin olive oil and chopped parsley. Serve with fresh lemons.

Serves 6

DEBONING WHOLE SOLE If you are using whole sole then you'll want to remove the bones after it is cooked. Keep in mind the bones are, in effect, really just one long spine and its projections, which make it a relatively simple matter to release the spine and remove all the bones at once. The slick and elegant way to do this is to first, using a fork, remove the head and tail and then trim away all but the edible fish so that what you have remaining is the bone sandwiched between the top and bottom fish filets. Insert the fork between the top fish filets and the bone and carefully separate the fish from the bones that run the length of the filet. Next insert the fork between the bone and the bottom fish filet and separate. At this point you, ideally, will have separated the bone completely from the top and bottom filets so that you can *slide* the fully intact bone sideways and remove it without disturbing the integrity of the fish.

Parmigiano-encrusted halibut over greens and beans

Greens and beans are an American-Italian restaurant staple, especially in Rochester, NY where they are practically obligatory. At *Mario's*, we start by toasting fresh chopped garlic in extra-virgin olive oil. Once the garlic has begun to brown, we add chopped shallots. We think this combination, *toasted* garlic and shallots, is the secret to great greens and beans. This pairing has been very popular at the restaurant.

PARMIGIANO-ENCRUSTED HALIBUT *6 portions halibut filets, 6-8 oz each* ‖ *3 cups panko (Japanese) style breadcrumbs* ‖ *2 oz parmigiano-reggiano or grana-padana cheese, freshly grated* ‖ *½ cup extra-virgin olive oil* ‖ *To taste, sea salt and freshly ground pepper* ‖ *1 lemon, cut into wedges*

GREEN AND BEANS *2 heads escarole, trimmed, washed, and cut* ‖ *1 cup extra-virgin olive oil* ‖ *2 tablespoons garlic, chopped* ‖ *4 shallots, chopped* ‖ *4-6 hot pepper pods* ‖ *1½ cup chicken broth, homemade (see page 61) or use canned broth* ‖ *2 (15.5 oz) cans cannellini beans, drained and rinsed* ‖ *To taste, Kosher salt and freshly ground pepper*

ONE For the greens and beans: Chop the escarole and blanch in boiling water for 1 minute or until tender. Drain, rinse under cold water, and set aside. **TWO** Heat the olive oil in a large sauté pan over medium-high heat. Add the garlic and fry to lightly toast to a golden brown color. Add the shallots and pepper pods and cook about 3 minutes or until the shallots are soft. Squeeze any excess moisture from the escarole and add to the pan together with the beans and the chicken broth. Season to taste with Kosher salt and freshly ground pepper. **THREE** To prepare the sea bass: Combine the breadcrumbs, cheese, and half of the olive oil. Coat the sea bass with the remaining oil and season to taste with salt and freshly ground pepper. Dredge the sea bass in the breadcrumb mixture to coat. Bake at 350° F for 20-25 minutes or until *just* done. Plate the beans and greens and top with the sea bass. Serve with lemon wedges.

Serves 6

THEY'RE NOT "BROWNS AND BEANS" For tender greens that are actually green and not bitter first, trim away any discolored leaves and cut about 2-2 ½ inches, the white part, off of the bottom. This is the where most of the bitterness comes from. Secondly, blanch the greens in ample water since escarole is naturally high in acid. It is this acid that causes them to turn brown and taste bitter so you need plenty of water to flush it out. Additionally, always bring the water to a rolling boil. The greens will cook more quickly this way and less cooking time means they are spending less time essentially bathing in acid. Lastly, drain, rinse with cold water and gently squeeze out the excess water. This squeezing will also help to remove the bitterness.

Grilled rainbow trout with Portobello mushrooms and sage-butter sauce

We make it a point to include fish that are recommended by the *Marine Stewardship Council*, the *Global Marine Program* and other sustainable fisheries initiatives on our menus. Trout is farm raised, which ensures sustainability, with farming methods that are also considered environmentally friendly. Trout also tastes quite good, particularly grilled, possessing one of the most unique flavors of all fish. This dish is on our banquet menu.

INGREDIENTS *6 Fresh rainbow trout, dressed ‖ 4-6 large Portobello mushrooms, washed as needed ‖ ½ cup fresh sage leaves, stripped from the stem ‖ 1 cup extra-virgin olive oil ‖ To taste, kosher salt and freshly ground black pepper*

SAGE-BUTTER SAUCE *½ cup fresh sage leaves, stripped from the stem ‖ 2 tablespoons extra-virgin olive oil ‖ 1 lemon, juiced ‖ 4 ounces unsalted butter ‖ ¼ cup water or chicken broth ‖ 2 ounces grana-padana or asiago cheese, grated ‖ To taste, sea salt and freshly ground black pepper*

ONE Remove the dorsal and side fins from the trout. Slice the mushrooms about ½ inch thick. **TWO** For the sage-butter sauce: Sauté the sage in 1 tablespoon of butter in a small saucepan over medium heat. Add the lemon juice and water or, for better flavor, chicken broth, and season to taste with salt and pepper. Whisk in the remaining butter and grated cheese. **THREE** Brush olive oil on the trout and mushroom slices and season them with salt and pepper to taste. Place the trout, skin side up onto a pre-heated char-grill together with the mushrooms. Cook, turning as needed for about five minutes or until the fish is *just* done and the mushrooms are tender. **FOUR** Remove the trout to a plate and place the mushrooms on the fish. Spoon some sauce on top. Serve with fresh lemon wedges (the optional garnish shown in the photo is slow-roasted seasoned tomato slices).

Serves 6

SAGE Sage, or *salvia*, has been cultivated in Italy for centuries where it grows wild together with thyme and rosemary. It's difficult not to notice the earthy, herbaceous aroma of these plants wafting through hillsides near the Italian coast. Sage is widely used in Italian veal, liver, and pork recipes like *saltimbocca*. It is one of those magical ingredients that can turn something ordinary into something special, transforming without overpowering.

Eggplant parmesan

Having its roots in the Abruzzi region of Italy, our eggplant parmesan is unlike anything you're likely to find on this side of the Atlantic. One key difference is the fact that it's layered in a baking dish and then cut into portions like you would a baked lasagna dish. It's also battered rather than breaded. This recipe was a staple at *Mario's Pizza & Pasta* and then later at both *Mario's* and *Bazil*.

INGREDIENTS *1 batch battered eggplant slices ‖ 1 lb mozzarella cheese, shredded ‖ 8 ounces parmigiano-reggiano or grana-padana cheese, grated ‖ ½ lb Swiss cheese, sliced ‖ 5 cups Abruzzi sauce (see page 5) or use Mario's marinara sauce (see page 2) or use 2 jars Mario's Pasta Sauce*

BATTERED EGGPLANT SLICES *5-6 large eggplants ‖ 1 quart whole milk ‖ 3 large eggs ‖ 9 cups all-purpose flour, sifted, then measured ‖ 5-6 cloves garlic, chopped ‖ ½ cup fresh basil, chopped ‖ To taste, Kosher salt and freshly ground pepper ‖ Additional salt for curing the eggplant ‖ Oil or frying shortening as needed to fry the eggplant*

ONE Prepare a batch of Abruzzi sauce, Mario's marinara sauce, or use 2 jars of Mario's Pasta Sauce. **TWO** Peel and slice the eggplant lengthwise about ⅜ inch thick. Lay the slices out on a wire rack and lightly salt them. Cover them with a towel and place in the refrigerator 6-8 hours or overnight. Eggplant contains bitter compounds, which are drawn out by the salt. **THREE** Mix the eggs and milk to combine in a large bowl. In a separate bowl, combine the flour, garlic, basil, salt, and pepper to taste. Add the dry mixture to the wet mixture and mix until smooth and not lumpy. **FOUR** Heat frying oil to 325° F using a deep fryer, electric wok, or a frying pan with a clip-on thermometer. Dredge the eggplant slices individually in the remaining flour and dip them into the batter, allowing the excess batter to drip. Fry on both sides for about 2 minutes each or until the batter turns golden brown and the eggplant is cooked. Lay the eggplant out on paper towels to allow the excess oil to be absorbed. **FIVE** Coat the bottom of a 9-by-12 inch casserole dish with a thin layer of sauce. Place an even layer of fried eggplant slices on the bottom of the dish. Spoon another layer of sauce on top of the eggplant and sprinkle a generous amount of mozzarella and grated cheese over the sauce. Repeat this process up to the top of the casserole dish, substituting one layer of mozzarella for one layer of Swiss cheese. **SIX** Cover with foil and bake at 350° F degrees for 15 minutes or until it is warm throughout and the cheese has melted. Remove the foil and top with additional sauce and cheese. Return to the oven to melt the cheese and serve with additional sauce on the side.

Serves 8

MARIO'S PASTA & PIZZA Mario Daniele opened his East Avenue location, *Mario's Pizza & Pasta*, in 1980. His recipes for marinara, Alfredo, and Abruzzi style fresh tomato sauces together with his hard crust herb rolls, authentic thin crust pizza, and dishes like this eggplant parmesan would become the cornerstone recipes of one of Rochester's most popular restaurants.

Dolci—
desserts and sweets

Men of Castelnuovo, Italy 1961

Merengata

This is one of our signature desserts. It's an unusual confection of crisp baked almond meringue layered with sweetened mascarpone and fresh raspberry sauce. We use rice flour in this recipe, which makes this a great gluten-free option for gluten sensitive guests but all-purpose flour works just as well.

INGREDIENTS *1 batch meringue discs ‖ 2 cups mascarpone cheese ‖ ½ cup confectionery sugar ‖ 1 (10 oz) package frozen raspberries, defrosted ‖ To taste, sugar ‖ 1 pint fresh raspberries ‖ Fresh mint, as needed for garnish*

MERINGUE DISCS *1¾ cup egg white ‖ 6 ½ oz sugar ‖ 2 oz confectionery sugar ‖ 4 oz blanched sliced almonds ‖ 1 oz rice flour (or all purpose flour)*

ONE Spread the almonds out onto a baking pan and toast them at 350 °F for about 8 minutes or until they turn golden brown. Set aside to cool. **TWO** Whip the egg whites in a clean, dry bowl on high speed until stiff peaks start to form. Slowly add the sugar, continuing to whip the whites into stiff peaks. **THREE** Once the almonds have cooled, transfer them to a food processor and pulse briefly to break them down into crumbles. Combine the almonds with the confectionery sugar and the rice flour. Fold the dry ingredients into the egg whites to complete the meringue. **FOUR** Put the meringue in a pastry bag fitted with a round tip. Line baking pans with parchment paper and pipe the meringue into 3-inch circles onto the paper. Bake for 2 hours in a preheated 250° F oven or until the discs lift easily off the paper. **FIVE** Place the frozen raspberries in a blender or food processor and blend or process until they are smooth. Add sugar to taste to sweeten. Strain the seeds out using a fine wire mesh strainer or cheesecloth. **SIX** To finish the dessert: Spread mascarpone onto the 3-4 discs and generously powder them with confectionery sugar. Finally, top with a dollop of raspberry sauce. Stack the finished discs and cap the stack with a plain disc. Repeat with the remaining discs. Decorate with additional confectionery sugar, fresh raspberries, and mint.

Serves 6

THANKS GRUMPY This dessert debuted in 1995 as a full sized torte, which had to be partially frozen and cut with piano wire before service. This proved to be difficult to handle since it would easily crumble plus the meringue would break down during the hot summer months due to humidity. We were losing more portions than we were actually selling so we decided to take it off the menu. A few years later Chef Keith "Grumpy" Killenbeck brought it back. Grumpy solved the problems we were having by baking small single portion sized meringue discs that could be easily stacked fresh to order. We've been making it Grumpy's way ever since. Grumpy also developed the Valentino mousse recipe in this book.

Lemon custard filled crepes with strawberry

Crepes, or *crespelle*, have been an important part of Italian cuisine since the French invasion during the eighteenth century, particularly in the Abruzzi region, where many simple and unusual recipes, both sweet and savory are centered around crepes.

INGREDIENTS *1 batch crepes* ‖ *1 batch lemon custard* ‖ *1 cup sugar* ‖ *1 pint fresh strawberries, stems removed and washed* ‖ *Assorted berries and fresh mint for garnish*

CREPES *3 large egg yolks* ‖ *1½ cups all-purpose flour, sifted then measured* ‖ *1 cup milk* ‖ *½ cup water* ‖ *5 tablespoons melted unsalted butter* ‖ *1 tablespoon sugar* ‖ *3 tablespoons, orange liquor, triple sec, or rum*

LEMON CUSTARD *1 cup sugar* ‖ *½ cup cornstarch* ‖ *½ teaspoon salt* ‖ *4 egg yolks* ‖ *1½ cups water* ‖ *Juice of 2-3 lemons* ‖ *4 tablespoons butter*

ONE For the crepes: Combine the milk, water, egg yolks, sugar, liquor, flour, and melted butter in a blender or food processor. Process until the mixture is well blended. Cover and refrigerate 2-3 hours or overnight. Heat a small non-stick omelet pan or crepe pan over medium-high heat until the pan becomes hot. Add a small amount of butter to the pan to keep the batter from sticking. Ladle or spoon a small amount of batter into the pan and allow it to spread into a thin layer about 4 inches in diameter. After the crepe begins to brown on the bottom, carefully turn it over and continue cooking for another 30 seconds or until the crepe is nicely browned. Remove the crepe and repeat the process until all of the batter is used up. **TWO** For the lemon custard: In a large saucepan or double boiler combine sugar, cornstarch, and salt. Mix well. Beat the egg yolks and water together, then whisk into sugar mixture. Cook over medium heat, stirring constantly, until mixture is thickened. Remove from heat and stir in lemon juice and butter. Cover with plastic wrap until completely cooled. **THREE** Process the strawberries in a blender or food processor until they are smooth. Add 1 tablespoon of sugar, or to taste. **FOUR** Spread the lemon custard onto each of the crepes and fold them in half. Spoon a circle of strawberry sauce onto a serving plate and place 2 crepes in the center of the circle so the sauce surrounds the crepes. Be careful not to sit the crepes directly in the sauce. **FIVE** Dust the crepes with an even layer of sugar and, using a crème brûlée torch, caramelize the sugar. Garnish with fresh berries and mint.

Serves 6

Apple-walnut tart

September through November is apple season in Western New York. In our opinion the variety and quality of apples grown here are unsurpassed anywhere in the world. This is the time of year when we use apples for all manner of preparations both sweet and savory. This classic Italian tart was developed by Michael Pergolini who was the first Executive Chef at *Mario's Via Abruzzi*.

SHORT DOUGH CRUST *2¾ cup all-purpose flour* ‖ *⅓ cup granulated sugar* ‖ *5 oz unsalted butter* ‖ *1 large egg* ‖ *Zest of one lemon, finely chopped*

APPLE FILLING *20-24 apples, medium* ‖ *1 cup granulated sugar* ‖ *2 tablespoons ground cinnamon* ‖ *¼ cup butter* ‖ *1 cup walnuts, shelled and chopped* ‖ *½ cup raisins*

CARAMEL SAUCE *7 oz corn syrup* ‖ *1 cup sugar* ‖ *1 cup heavy whipping cream* ‖ *½ cup water*

ONE For the short dough: Sift the flour and then measure it. Mix the flour and sugar. Cut the butter into pea-sized cubes and incorporate into the flour mixture. Once the butter is incorporated, form a ball. Wrap and chill for 30 minutes. **TWO** For the apple filling: Toss apples, sugar, and cinnamon into a bowl. Melt butter in a large skillet. Add the apples and sauté until the apples are *just* tender. Set aside to cool. Drain and return them to the bowl with walnuts and raisins. **THREE** For the caramel sauce: Bring the water and sugar to a boil. Add corn syrup and bring to a second boil. Continue to boil until the syrup becomes caramelized. Carefully remove from the heat and slowly add the heavy cream. The mixture will be quite hot so use caution when handling. **FOUR** To assemble the pie: Roll out the dough to line a two-piece 10-inch fluted pan. Add the apple mixture. Peel and slice an additional 10-12 apples and fan them decoratively around the top of the tart. Brush with additional melted butter and sprinkle generously with granulated sugar. Bake at 325° F for 20-25 minutes or until golden brown. Serve with warm caramel sauce.

Makes 1 pie

WHAT APPLES ARE BEST TO USE? For this tart or other pies, we recommend using the seasonal, locally grown Macoun and Jonagold apples. If these are not available, use Empire apples, which are good all-purpose apples. Avoid McIntosh and Cortland apples, as they tend to break down upon cooking.

Tiramisu

Ask someone to name the first Italian dessert that comes to mind and the answer will most likely be tiramisu or cannoli. Considering tiramisu's iconic status it's almost hard to believe that it was only as recent as the late 1960's that food historians generally agree the dessert was first created in Northern Italy. Despite the fact that a recipe for tiramisu did not appear in a cookbook until 1983, nearly every Italian restaurant in America had it on the dessert menu by the end of the decade.

INGREDIENTS *1 lb mascarpone cheese* ‖ *6 eggs, separated* ‖ *6 tablespoons granulated sugar* ‖ *1 cup heavy (whipping) cream* ‖ *½ cup light rum* ‖ *2 cups strong espresso (Italian) coffee, cold* ‖ *8 oz chocolate flavored coffee syrup* ‖ *24 ladyfingers (savoiardi)* ‖ *½ cup cocoa powder (Dutch process cocoa)* ‖ *2 oz chocolate shavings* ‖ *Fresh mixed berries for garnish*

ONE Make 2 cups espresso. Add the chocolate coffee syrup to the espresso. **TWO** Separate the eggs. Whip the whites in a clean dry bowl with a scant amount of sugar until they reach the stiff peak stage. Transfer to the refrigerator. Whip the yolks on high speed for 2 minutes. Add the remaining sugar to the yolks and continue to mix on high speed until the yolks are at the ribbon stage. This should take about about 1 additional minute. **THREE** Add the mascarpone to the egg yolk mixture and mix in at low speed. Gradually add the heavy cream to the mixture and mix in at low speed. Once the cream has been incorporated, turn the mixer up to medium speed, and whip until it starts to slightly thicken. Do not over whip. Gently fold the whites into the mixture. Do not over mix, as this will cause the egg whites to destabilize. **FOUR** Dip ladyfingers into the espresso mixture. Place a single layer on the bottom of a 9-by-12 inch, glass dish or glass trifle bowl. Drizzle some rum over them and sprinkle with cocoa powder. Pour a layer, about half, of the mascarpone mixture evenly over the ladyfingers. Repeat step four and top with additional cocoa powder and chocolate shavings. **FIVE** Cover and refrigerate overnight at least 8 hours to allow the tiramisu to set.

Serves 8-10

PICK ME UP! *Tiramisu* or *Tira Mi Su* literally means "pick-me-up" in Italian. This is because of the supposed lift you get from the espresso that the ladyfingers are soaked in. This sounds about right to us considering you are eating the equivalent of one serving of espresso per serving of tiramisu.

Mascarpone and lavender crème brûlée

Lavender has become something of a culinary darling in recent years. Possessing a truly unique and delicate flavor that almost defies description, lavender is best appreciated in delicate dishes like this one, where there are no other strong competing flavors. This recipe was created at *Mario's*.

INGREDIENTS *3½ cups heavy (whipping) cream* ‖ *¼ cup milk* ‖ *1 tablespoon dried lavender flowers* ‖ *1 vanilla bean split in half lengthwise* ‖ *4 egg yolks* ‖ *2 eggs* ‖ *½ cup instant dissolving sugar* ‖ *1½ cup mascarpone cheese* ‖ *3 tablespoons brown sugar*

ONE In a large, heavy saucepan over medium heat, add cream, vanilla bean and lavender flowers. Heat to a simmer. Remove from heat and allow lavender flowers to steep, like tea, into the cream for 5 minutes. Strain cream mixture through a fine mesh strainer to remove lavender flowers and vanilla bean. **TWO** In a suitably sized saucepan, whisk together the egg yolks, eggs, and sugar until light and creamy. Gradually add the mascarpone, whisking constantly. **THREE** Slowly add the strained cream to the egg mixture, blending well. Place over low heat, whisking constantly, until the mixture thickens and coats the back of a spoon. **FOUR** Pour the crème mixture into crème brulèe dishes, custard cups, or glasses. Transfer to a refrigerator to set overnight. **FIVE** Dust the surfaces evenly with sugar. A whisper thin layer is all you need. Use a crème brûlée torch to caramelize the sugar. Decorate the top with a few additional lavender leaves.

Serves 6

COOKING WITH LAVENDER If you decide to experiment with lavender, keep in mind that a little goes a long way. It will be like eating perfume and will turn a dish bitter if too much is used. If fresh lavender is not available, use dry lavender but only use about a third as much as you would fresh. Lavender can replace rosemary or thyme in many recipes. It adds an element of *mysterioso* to everything from bread to ice cream.

Pumpkin, custard, and ricotta cheesecake

Italian cheesecake fillings are made with ricotta cheese which means they differ somewhat from the cream cheese based New York style cheesecakes that most of us are used to. Simply put, ricotta based fillings are lighter, less dense and not at all tangy like cream cheese fillings. This filling also calls for custard and pumpkin, an ingredient that is used more often in everyday Italian cooking than it is in America except, of course, during the holiday season, which is when we like to feature this cheesecake.

PIE DOUGH *2 cups all-purpose flour, sifted then measured ‖ ¼ cup sugar ‖ ½ cup unsalted butter ‖ 3 tablespoons vegetable shortening, chilled ‖ 1 large egg ‖ ½-¾ cup ice water*

CUSTARD *4 egg yolks ‖ ¾ cup sugar ‖ 3 tablespoons flour, sifted then measured ‖ 2 cups milk ‖ 2 teaspoons vanilla extract*

PUMPKIN-RICOTTA FILLING *1½ cup fresh ricotta ‖ 1 tablespoon cocoa powder ‖ ¼ cup sugar ‖ ¼ teaspoon ground cinnamon ‖ ½ teaspoon ground nutmeg ‖ 1 cup pie pumpkin or canned pumpkin for pie filling*

ONE For the dough: Mix the flour and sugar in a food processor or mixing bowl, as needed to combine. Add the butter and shortening and mix to obtain a cornmeal-like texture. Add the egg and mix to blend. Slowly add the water, a few drops at a time, until the dough begins to form. Remove the dough and shape into a ball. Wrap and chill for at least 1 hour. **TWO** For the custard: Put the yolks, sugar, and flour into a saucepan and whisk until smooth. Add cold milk and vanilla. Continuously whisk over medium heat until the mixture thickens. Do not boil. When the mixture has thickened, chill completely. **THREE** Peel a small pumpkin and cut into large cubes. Steam the pumpkin using a vegetable steamer until the pumpkin cooks throughout. Purée in a food processor. Put the pumpkin purée in a wire mesh strainer and allow it to drain overnight. Alternatively, use canned pumpkin. Mix the pumpkin together with the remaining filling ingredients. **FOUR** To assemble the pie: Butter a 10 inch fluted two-pieced tart pan. Cut the dough in half, set one half aside, and roll out the other half to fill the tart pan. Fold the custard into the ricotta mixture and pour into the shell. Roll out the reserve dough and cut into ¼ inch strips. Crisscross the strips to form a lattice top. Bake at 350° F for about 1 hour or until firm. Chill completely before serving.

Makes 1 cheesecake

THIS IS NOT NEW YORK STYLE Italians have been making cheesecake since pre-Roman times when it was adopted from the Greeks. It wasn't until the later half of the 19th century that cream cheese as we know was first manufactured in upstate New York. This would lead to the development of New York style cheesecake.

Pears cooked in Marsala and stuffed with mascarpone

In Italy dessert often consists simply of fruit perhaps accompanied with fresh cheese or a simple dish made with cooked fruit like this one. We recommend Bosc pears when poaching because they have a distinctive elegant shape with a long tapered neck and unblemished yellow-brown skin allowing for the best possible presentation. They also keep their shape after poaching which is equally important. Use a toothpick and check them often for doneness, as soon as you can easily pierce the pears they are done.

INGREDIENTS *6 large pears, Bosc* ‖ *1 (750 ml) bottle sweet Marsala wine* ‖ *4 cups granulated sugar* ‖ *6-8 star anise* ‖ *2 cups mascarpone cheese* ‖ *2 tablespoons heavy (whipping) cream* ‖ *Water, enough to cover the pears*

ONE Mix the mascarpone with the heavy cream, ¼ cup Marsala wine and 3 tablespoons of sugar. **TWO** Peel the pears and, using a paring knife or melon baller, core them from the bottom. Place the pears in a non-reactive pan with the rest of the Marsala, the remaining sugar, the star anise, and enough water to just barely cover the pears. Simmer covered for about 20 minutes. At this point, check for doneness using a toothpick. The pears are done when you can easily pierce them with the toothpick. Continue to simmer or until the pears are *just* cooked throughout. Remove the pears and chill completely. Reserve the poaching liquid. **THREE** Bring the reserve poaching liquid to a boil over high heat and cook down until it reaches a syrup consistency that will coat the back of a spoon. This simple syrup will be used to the sauce the pear. **FOUR** Fill the pears with the mascarpone mixture. Serve with the syrup from the poaching liquid and a dollop of the remaining cheese mixture.

Serves 6

IT'S NOT MARSCAPONE! That's right, it's not mars-capone! It's mas-carpone! Don't feel bad if you've been saying it wrong, most people do, we've even heard Iron Chefs mispronounce it! Now you know and while we're at it, we'd also like to point out that it's bal-samic vinegar, not ba-salmic vinegar.

Sweet ricotta ravioli

Think of these ravioli as kind-of-like a warm cannoli. Like cannoli these ricotta cheese, sugar and cinnamon filled pasta are crispy fried and then dusted generously with confectionery sugar. Sounds good right? Street vendors sell these all over Italy especially in Abruzzi and Sicily, where it is traditional to serve them around Christmas time. We serve them as full dessert with strawberry sauce and fresh berries but they are also a great snack for any time.

INGREDIENTS *2 lb ricotta cheese* ‖ *1 cup, plus 1 tablespoon, granulated sugar* ‖ *¼ teaspoon ground cinnamon* ‖ *6 egg whites* ‖ *½ cup confectionery sugar* ‖ *1 pint fresh strawberries* ‖ *Fresh assorted berries as needed* ‖ *1 batch basic pasta dough (see page 76)*

ONE Prepare the ravioli filling by mixing the ricotta with 1 cup sugar, cinnamon, and egg whites **TWO** Prepare 1 batch of pasta dough. Prepare the pasta sheets using a hand-cranked pasta sheeter set on a thin setting. Lay the dough out on a ravioli tray and fill the pockets with the sweet ricotta filling according to the manufacturer's instructions. **THREE** Prepare the strawberry sauce by removing the stems from the berries and washing them. Transfer them to purée in a food processor or blender with 1 tablespoon of sugar to sweeten. Process or blend until smooth. **FOUR** Heat frying oil to 350° F using a deep fryer, electric wok, or a frying pan with a clip-on thermometer. Fry the ravioli until the dough becomes golden brown and crisp. **FIVE** Serve promptly with a generous dusting of confectionery sugar, the strawberry sauce, and assorted fresh berries.

Serves 6

HOW ABOUT RASPBERRY PASTA! Another popular fried pasta dessert from our menu is Raspberry Fettuccine where we make fresh pasta flavored with raspberry powder. The fried pasta is plated with a scoop of vanilla bean ice cream, white chocolate shavings, fresh berries and raspberry sauce. Yum!

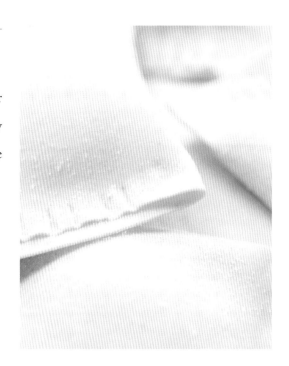

Valentino mousse

Layered chocolate and white chocolate mousse. This has been a staple on our dessert cart for many years. Try as we might, we just can't get rid of it. People keep asking for it back when we don't make it and complaining every time we run out of it. We suppose this is a good thing. As is true for all recipes, to get best results you'll need to use good quality ingredients, in this case good quality chocolate is a must. We use callets, or small chocolate discs, about the size of a dime, which are much easier to work with than block chocolate.

INGREDIENTS *12 oz semi-sweet chocolate callets* ‖ *12 oz white chocolate callets* ‖ *1½ cups whole milk* ‖ *6 cups heavy cream* ‖ *3 oz shaved chocolate* ‖ *Assorted berries and fresh mint for garnish*

ONE Gently heat the whole milk in a pot just below simmering. Do not boil the milk, as it will scald. **TWO** Put the milk chocolate and white chocolate into two separate metal bowls. Add 4 ounces of the milk to each bowl. Warm the chocolate mixtures by placing the bowls over a suitably sized pot that has about 1 inch of water in it. Simmer the water over low to moderate heat and stir until the chocolate has fully melted and smooth. **THREE** Allow the chocolate to cool to room temperature, or slightly less, by putting the mixtures in the refrigerator and mixing every few minutes. Do not allow the chocolate to harden. **FOUR** While the chocolate is cooling, whip the cream. The cream should be whipped until it is stiff but not to the point where it becomes granular in texture. **FIVE** When the chocolate has cooled to room temperature, gently fold half the whipped cream into each bowl. Mix until the chocolate has *just* blended evenly into the whipped cream. Take care not to over mix, as this will cause the cream to destabilize. **SIX** Refrigerate the mousse for 3-4 hours to allow it to set. Spoon or pipe the mousse from a pastry bag into glasses, alternating the white and dark layers. Garnish with chocolate shavings, fresh mint, and fresh berries.

Serves 6-8

Strawberry granita with vodka & candied lemon

Simple, yet elegant, this refreshing dessert has never failed to be a crowd pleaser at *Mario's*. In this recipe we blend Italian style lemon ice with fresh strawberries, cream and vodka. Feel free to go free-style and use other fruits such as mango, peach or raspberry instead of the strawberries. Sparkling wines, dessert wines and grappa are nice alternatives to the vodka.

INGREDIENTS *3 cups Italian lemon ice* ‖ *3 cups fresh strawberries, washed and tops removed* ‖ *½ cup heavy cream* ‖ *Vodka to taste* ‖ *2 fresh lemons* ‖ *Water as needed* ‖ *½ cup sugar* ‖ *Additional berries and fresh mint for garnish*

ONE For the candied lemon garnish: Use a paring knife or peeler to thinly peel the rind from the lemons, taking care to ensure that no pith (white part) is left on the peel. Slice the peel into thin julienne strips. Place in a small saucepan and cover with about 1 cup water. Bring to a boil and strain. Return the rind to the empty saucepan. Cover with about 1-cup fresh water and ½ cup sugar. Slowly bring to a boil, and then reduce the heat to very low. Simmer over very low heat until the water has cooked down and nothing but syrup and rind strips remain. Remove the lemon peels from the syrup and reserve for garnish. **TWO** Put the lemon ice and strawberries in a blender or food processor and blend or process until smooth. Add the cream and blend on high speed for 30 seconds. Add vodka to taste, taking care to not over dilute the mixture with vodka (although the final texture can be anything from stiff to somewhat loose depending upon your preference). **THREE** Pour the mixture into serving glasses and decorate with freshly chopped berries and candied lemon.

Serves 6-8

THANKS DAVIDE! Mario met Davide Bernardi through a friend in Italy, and the next thing we knew he was here working with us. A recent graduate of an Italian culinary school in Italy, he was looking to add *Mario's* to his resume. We wasted no time picking his brain when, on his very first day, we had him design a menu for an important gala dinner at the *Italian American Community Center* where he was introduced as our Guest Chef. He stayed with us for six months in 2006 (speaking virtually no English but he stuck it out with us anyway) and in the end it was a great experience having him at *Mario's*. This recipe and the recipe for Lemon Custard Crepes *(see page 193)* came from Davide.

Index

About the Author

Paul Maytan Jr. was the Executive Chef at Mario's for 16 years. As a self-described "imposter" he started learning his craft at the highly touted *Arizona Inn* in Tucson, Arizona and later at *Hyatt Regency* where he developed a culinary training program and was part of the Culinary Olympic Team at the Grand Hyatt in Atlanta during the 1996 Olympic Games. As Executive Chef of Mario's he twice traveled to Central Italy to study the cuisine, was featured at the James Beard House in Manhattan, and authored Mario's first cookbook *Mario's Via Abruzzi-The Cookbook*. He resides in Rochester with his wife Jackie and daughters Chloe and Eilish.

Author Acknowledgments

While this book was not put together with the usual army of editors, food stylists, designers and other contributors, many people have helped make this book possible.

Anthony Daniele, who wrote the forward and whose vision and support ultimately made this effort possible.

Photographers, Matt Wittmeyer and Sharon Merisola Yockel.

Proofreaders, Ashley Manchester and Janet Infarinato.

The talented chefs whose ideas and recipes are included in this book. Far too many names to list here but they are all given due props in the text.

The amazing Gary Butler and the other good folks at Phoenix Graphics who helped us achieve our vision.